What People Are Saying About Apostle Guillermo Maldonado and His Books...

My friend Apostle Guillermo Maldonado brilliantly prepares you to be part of God's end-time remnant. It is one minute to midnight. Time is running out!

—*Sid Roth*
Host, *It's Supernatural!*

The Holy Spirit gave Apostle Guillermo Maldonado this very powerful revelation of *End-Time Shaking and Revival*. It is truly a blessed book—a vision of things that are coming to pass to prepare the church for what is taking place in these last days. Apostle Maldonado is greatly anointed by the Holy Spirit to demonstrate the glory of God to this generation. You need to read *End-Time Shaking and Revival* and get ready for manifestations of God's great power in your church and in your life. You will be blessed by a divine encounter with God's power and glory.

—*Prophet Glenda Jackson*
Author, *Walking in Prophecy, Signs, and Wonders*

My friend Apostle Guillermo Maldonado is one of the most important voices in America and beyond. His passion for Jesus is contagious. He speaks with great authority and wisdom as he lives acutely aware of the times in which we are living as the church in this world. I highly recommend this faithful servant of the Lord and the message he carries for us all.

—*Bill Johnson*
Bethel Church, Redding, CA
Author of numerous books, including *When Heaven Invades Earth* and *The Way of Life*

T0053955

In *Jesus Is Coming Soon*, Apostle Guillermo Maldonado stresses, "This generation is on the verge of seeing the greatest outpouring of the Holy Spirit and the greatest revival in history. The remnant church is about to enter into the glory of God…. The earth began with the glory of God manifested in creation, and it will end with the glory manifested in the supernatural wonders of the last days, which God is about to reveal." This book shows how you can participate in God's greatest revival and see the manifestations of His glory during these momentous last days before the return of Jesus Christ!

—*Paula White-Cain*
Paula White Ministries
Evangelist and Senior Pastor
New Destiny Christian Center, Orlando, FL

I love Guillermo Maldonado and his passion to bring back the urgency of Christ's return as a central focus of the church. So many Christians are consumed with living out a destiny now without any regard to living for our eternal destiny: being with Jesus where He is. As he shares his perspective, Guillermo always points to eternity, and this causes people to have greater hope than if they were just hearing about how to live out their salvation in this turbulent world. We need the higher focus of our everlasting life motivating us in the now. We also need Jesus to be the center of this eternal focus, and *Jesus Is Coming Soon* helps to reframe our view while also guiding us like a compass. There are so many different perspectives about how Jesus will return and what that day will look like. Even if your theological perspective differs, I encourage you to read this book to gain new passion and live with eternity in view in your everyday life.

—*Shawn Bolz*
Host, *Translating God* television program
Host, *Exploring the Prophetic* podcast
Author, *Translating God*, *God Secrets*, and *Through the Eyes of Love*
www.bolzministries.com

Jesus Is Coming Soon is an important book. Many people are confused about basic biblical truth. The reality is that Jesus is coming soon, just as Apostle Maldonado clearly states. Because of this fact, reaching the world for Christ is one of our central mandates. One simply cannot read this book without finding one's heart burning for lost souls as well as longing for our Savior's return.

—*Cindy Jacobs*
Generals International

Your life has significance because you were created by God with a purpose. One fundamental task we have as believers is to discover our purpose. But another important assignment is to learn how to *achieve* that purpose. In his book *Created for Purpose*, Apostle Guillermo Maldonado clearly explains the process that is necessary to make it all the way to the finish line of a successful life!

—*Dr. Rod Parsley*
Pastor and founder, World Harvest Church, Columbus, OH

Believers sometimes run aimlessly through life with no true compass to guide them in their journey. Not knowing our purpose is one of the worst situations we can be in. But finally, there is no longer an excuse! Apostle Guillermo Maldonado has given us a blueprint for discovering and becoming all that God has created us to be. *Created for Purpose* will help equip thousands of believers in Christ Jesus to fulfill their God-ordained destiny!

—*Dr. James W. Goll*
Author, speaker, communications trainer, and recording artist
God Encounters Ministries

Apostle Guillermo Maldonado has been a spiritual son to me for many years. He is one of the most committed believers I have ever known, and frankly, he is a spiritual genius. His book *Created for Purpose* demonstrates how we are all concerned about understanding our destiny and having a clear vision, and I know the keys in this book will give you great assurance in these vital areas of your life.

—*Marilyn Hickey*
Marilyn Hickey Ministries

Apostle Guillermo Maldonado is leading an incredibly powerful movement of God across the globe. I've had the honor of witnessing his love of and devotion to the presence of God, which cultivate an atmosphere for the Lord to move in signs, wonders, and miracles. His ministry has touched countless lives with the redemptive power of Jesus!

His new book, *Breakthrough Prayer*, is written with a spirit of excellence, a mark of everything Maldonado puts his hands to. This book is a representation of his drive and passion for the bride of Christ to be prepared for and partner with what Jesus wants to do on the earth. In its pages, you will not find empty words to recite to God, but rather divine insight and activation into two-way communication with the Father.

—*Kris Vallotton*
Senior Associate Leader, Bethel Church, Redding, CA
Cofounder, Bethel School of Supernatural Ministry

Breakthrough Prayer is an outstanding book on the preciousness and power of prayer. In this wonderful new book, you will be instructed in how to build a personal relationship with Father God. Without question, you will gain much-needed insights into the priority of sincere prayer, and you will be taught how to enter into the secret place of prayer. Your life will be enriched as you study the profound insights from this book, and you will learn how to grow in prayer, moving into a higher spiritual realm. God moves when we pray! Remember, through prayer, we are forging the future and shaping the now. Don't waste any time—get this book and start your spiritual journey towards a deeper, more committed prayer life.

—*Bobby Conner*
Eagles View Ministries

Apostle Maldonado is an anointed vessel of God. His message is from the Holy Spirit, and Apostle is full of insight and revelation. He is gifted at bringing out hidden truths. Your spiritual walk with the Lord will be greatly enhanced after reading this book.

—*Dr. Don Colbert, MD*
New York Times best-selling author

END-TIME SHAKING AND REVIVAL

END-TIME SHAKING AND REVIVAL

BEST-SELLING AUTHOR
GUILLERMO MALDONADO

WHITAKER
HOUSE

Unless otherwise indicated, all Scripture quotations are taken from the *New King James Version*, © 1979, 1980, 1982 by Thomas Nelson, Inc. Used by permission. Scripture quotations marked (NIV) are taken from the *Holy Bible, New International Version*®, NIV®, © 1973, 1978, 1984, 2011 by Biblica, Inc.® Used by permission. All rights reserved worldwide. The "NIV" and "New International Version" are trademarks registered in the United States Patent and Trademark Office by Biblica, Inc.®

Boldface type in the Scripture quotations indicates the author's emphasis.
The forms LORD and GOD (in small caps) in Bible quotations represent the Hebrew name for God *Yahweh* (Jehovah), while *Lord* and *God* normally represent the name *Adonai*, in accordance with the Bible version used.

Definitions of Hebrew and Greek words are taken from the electronic version of *Strong's Exhaustive Concordance of the Bible*, STRONG (© 1980, 1986, and assigned to World Bible Publishers, Inc. Used by permission. All rights reserved.).

Pew Research Center bears no responsibility for the analyses or interpretations of its data presented in this book. The opinions expressed herein, including any implications for policy, are those of the author and not of Pew Research Center.

ERJ Credits:
Editor: Jose M. Anhuaman
Editorial Development: Gloria Zura
Translation: Vanesa Vargas
Cover Design: Danielle Cruz-Nieri

END-TIME SHAKING AND REVIVAL

Guillermo Maldonado
13651 S.W. 143rd Ct., #101 • Miami, FL 33186
http://kingjesusministry.org/
www.ERJPub.org

ISBN: 978-1-64123-770-3 • eBook ISBN: 978-1-64123-771-0
Printed in the United States of America
© 2021 by Guillermo Maldonado

Whitaker House
1030 Hunt Valley Circle • New Kensington, PA 15068
www.whitakerhouse.com

Library of Congress Control Number: 2021945479

1 2 3 4 5 6 7 8 9 10 11 ⨆ 28 27 26 25 24 23 22 21

CONTENTS

FIRST SHAKING, THEN REVIVAL: THE ORDER OF THE END-TIME CYCLE

The Scriptures teach us that there is an order, or sequence, in which God's end-time plans will unfold: shaking will precede revival, and then revival will bring about the greatest harvest of souls for Christ ever witnessed, even as the shaking continues. In God's sovereign purposes, we can't enter into revival without first experiencing shaking. But many people are confused and fearful about the shaking because they don't understand the order or the significance of the end-time cycle.

Seeking guidance from the Holy Spirit, I have written *End-Time Shaking and Revival* to help the church and the world discern the meaning of the unprecedented shakings happening on earth today and to reveal how we can participate in God's last-days manifestations of glory. I expand on end-times themes I introduced in my previous books, explaining how to respond correctly to divine shakings, be continuously filled with the Spirit, participate in the worldwide revival, and move in the supernatural.

During the end-times revival, we will be exposed to various facets of the power of the Holy Spirit, including growing manifestations of His light and intensity—the revelation of God's truth and holiness—along with signs and wonders. Revival will simultaneously erupt in different places around the world, creating tremendous global impact. In the final part of the revival, we will see the beginning of God's judgment on the world. Then Jesus, in His glory, will appear for His remnant church, and the world will undergo the great tribulation. (See Matthew 24:21.) These events will lead to what the Bible calls *"the fullness of the times"* (Ephesians 1:10)—the culminating events of Jesus's second coming, His reign on earth during the millennium, and the final judgment of those who have not believed in God and His Son Jesus.

END-TIME SHAKING

As the Bible tells us, no one knows the day or the hour when Jesus will appear for His church (see Matthew 24:36), because His arrival will be sudden, abrupt, and when we least expect it: *"For you yourselves know perfectly that the day of the Lord so comes as a thief in the night"* (1 Thessalonians 5:2). However, as I indicated above, we can analyze the order of these events that will culminate in Jesus's second coming to earth.

First, I want to establish this fundamental truth: all the disturbances that are happening around us, and that are causing people so much consternation, are signs from God pointing to the coming of the Lord. As we draw closer to the end, we will see these signs intensify and become more frequent and evident.

Second, we know that God Himself is behind the shaking because He told us through His prophet Haggai, and in other biblical passages, that it would occur:

> For thus says the LORD of hosts: "Once more (it is a little while) I will shake heaven and earth, the sea and dry land; and I will shake all nations, and they shall come to the Desire of All Nations, and I will fill this temple with glory," says the LORD of hosts. "The silver is Mine, and the gold is Mine," says the LORD of hosts. "The glory of this latter temple shall be greater than the former," says the LORD of hosts. "And in this place I will give peace," says the LORD of hosts.
>
> (Haggai 2:6–9)

Prophecy in the Bible gives us revelation regarding three groups: Israel, the church, and the world. God loves the people of each group, and they all have a part in His plan for the human race at the end of time. He chose Israel to be a priesthood to the world, and He adopted the gentiles into His family with the coming of Jesus. However, those who have rejected Him entirely—from both groups—are called "the world" because they are living contrary to His divine purposes.

It is important to understand that the above prophecy from Haggai refers to all three groups, but in different ways. Each group is processed in a distinct manner during shakings. The shaking of the church is different from the shaking of Israel or the world. The shaking of the church is for purification, the shaking of Israel is for salvation, and the shaking of the world is for judgment—and, if people yield to God, for repentance. Each group will experience shaking, and the results will bring glory to the Lord. The remnant church will be filled with God's glory and demonstrate His signs and wonders, the Jews will begin to acknowledge their Messiah in greater numbers, and many people in the world will recognize that God alone has the answers to their dilemmas and distress.

PERIL IN THE COSMOS

As the end-time shaking progresses, there will be peril in the cosmos. We read in the book of Isaiah, "*Therefore* **I will shake the heavens, and the earth will move out of her place**, *in the wrath of the* Lord *of hosts and in the day of His fierce anger*" (Isaiah 13:13). God has shown me that there will be turmoil in the cosmos, and this revelation is confirmed by what He has previously announced through His Word. In this century, wars between nations will be particularly fought in outer space. Russia, China, and other nations appear to be arming with the intent of conducting space warfare against the United States' military and communications satellites.[1] In 2019, the United States formed the U.S. Space Force (USSF) "in order to protect U.S. and allied interests in space and to provide space capabilities to the joint force,"[2] recognizing that if it can successfully protect its satellite capability from attack by other nations, it will maintain its military strength on the earth.[3]

---

1. "EEUU planifica una guerra cósmica contra Rusia y China" ["The US Plans a Cosmic War Against Russia and China"], October 24, 2016, https://www.hispantv.com/noticias/eeuu-/312107/guerra-cosmica-satelites-rusia-china.
2. "USSF Mission," United States Space Force, https://www.spaceforce.mil/About-Us/About-Space-Force/Mission/.
3. Chris Bowlby, "Could a War in Space Really Happen?" BBC News, December 19, 2015, https://www.bbc.com/news/magazine-35130478.

But warfare against satellites isn't the only peril involving the cosmos. NASA studies are predicting that in 2029, an asteroid called Apophis will pass very close to the earth, less than 20,000 miles, although calculations in 2004 predicted that it would collide with our planet.[4] The asteroid was named Apophis in reference to an "ancient Egyptian spirit of evil, darkness and destruction."[5] It will pass closer than the distance of some satellites, and since it is still a number of years off, it's not clear whether the earth is fully out of danger of impact. Recently, we have seen the shaking of nature and other arenas on earth, although we have not yet seen it in space. We may see a preview of this before the rapture of the church.

The prophet Thomas Horn—who predicted the resignation of Pope Benedict XVI[6]—recently had a night vision in which he saw what looked like a giant, fiery dragon moving like a snake and coming straight down to earth. Suddenly, his perspective changed, and he was able see from above and discover that this apparent dragon was actually an asteroid moving and shining in the sunlight. His perspective switched back to earth again, and he was on a mountain with thousands and thousands of other people who were running for their lives, screaming in desperation, and asking God to save them. Next, he saw that giant, burning rock enter the atmosphere and break into pieces that fell in different places. The earth began to shake violently, and it sounded like the world was coming apart. No one could stay standing. An enormous section of the asteroid had fallen into the sea, causing a huge tsunami with waves hundreds of feet tall that flooded over the top of the mountain.

Thomas said that, after this, what felt like large hands lifted him up into space. Looking down, he saw the seawater boiling, volcanoes erupting, and tremendous hurricanes breaking out. When he woke up, he nearly fell out of bed because the vision had been so vivid and had felt so real.

---

4. "NASA Analysis: Earth Is Safe from Asteroid Apophis for 100-Plus Years," Asteroids, NASA, March 26, 2021, https://www.nasa.gov/feature/jpl/nasa-analysis-earth-is-safe-from-asteroid-apophis-for-100-plus-years.
5. J. Hill, "Apep (Apophis)," Ancient Egypt Online, 2010, https://ancientegyptonline.co.uk/apep/.
6. Tom Horn and Cris Putnam, "The Final Pope & Project Lucifer," interview with Sid Roth, *It's Supernatural!*, YouTube video, 22:52, March 31, 2013, https://www.youtube.com/watch?v=VTmgmJ_PfIE.

As he recovered and began to write down what he had seen, it was if he heard a voice, whether out loud or in his head, saying a name: *Apophis*[7]. In Revelation 8:10–11, the Bible speaks of a star called Wormwood that will fall on a third of the waters and cause many people to die:

> *Then the third angel sounded: and a great star fell from heaven, burning like a torch, and it fell on a third of the rivers and on the springs of water. The name of the star is Wormwood. A third of the waters became wormwood, and many men died from the water, because it was made bitter.*

In the last days, asteroids will fall on the earth and make our planet move off its axis. When the shaking of the cosmos occurs, all communication signals will be interrupted. *"Immediately after the tribulation of those days the sun will be darkened, and the moon will not give its light; the stars will fall from heaven, and the powers of the heavens will be shaken"* (Matthew 24:29). The tribulation that Jesus refers to here is not the great tribulation at the end of the age but rather the shaking that precedes the coming end-time revival. Famine, pestilence, pandemics, plagues, floods, fires, tsunamis, hurricanes, earthquakes, and much more will occur at the same time. John described all this in a vision he recorded in Revelation:

> *So I looked, and behold, a pale horse. And the name of him who sat on it was Death, and Hades followed with him. And power was given to them over a fourth of the earth, to kill with sword, with hunger, with death, and by the beasts of the earth. When He opened the fifth seal, I saw under the altar the souls of those who had been slain for the word of God and for the testimony which they held. And they cried with a loud voice, saying, "How long, O Lord, holy and true, until You judge and avenge our blood on those who dwell on the earth?" Then a white robe was given to each of them; and it was said to them that they should rest a little while longer, until both the number of their fellow servants and their brethren, who would be killed as they were, was completed.*
>
> (Revelation 6:8–11)

---

7. Tom Horn, interview with Sid Roth, *It's Supernatural!*, 28:30, March 8, 2020, https://sidroth.org/television/tv-archives/tom-horn-2/.

SIGNS OF THE END TIMES

Today, this shaking is already happening before our eyes. For example, as I write this book, we are experiencing one of the greatest pandemics in the last hundred years, COVID-19. The website Worldometer records that, as of August 6, 2021, there were over 202 million cases and nearly 4.3 million deaths.[8]

In 2020, the United Nations declared that the plague of locusts affecting Africa was "the most dangerous migratory epidemic in the world." These insects left millions of people in a food emergency.[9] The brush fires in Australia during 2019–2020 as a result of climate change were of a magnitude that was not expected until the next century. Entire ecosystems disappeared under the flames. Between July 2019 and February 2020, 37,500 square miles (97,000 square kilometers) of forest were burned.[10] Additional environmental, social, economic, political, and personal shaking are occurring and will occur in the world.

THE SIGNS OF CHRIST'S APPEARING ARE SHAKING, REVIVAL, AND THE HARVESTING OF SOULS.

END-TIME REVIVAL AND HARVEST

During a shaking, God introduces the Holy Spirit to His people in a greater way. He pours His the Spirit onto those who fervently seek His infilling. The outpouring of the Holy Spirit in the end times will be more powerful than that which occurred at the beginning of the church. It will be the prelude to Christ's appearing because, as I mentioned previously, it

8. https://www.worldometers.info/coronavirus/.
9. "La plaga de langostas es la epidemia migratoria más peligrosa del mundo" ["The Locust Plague Is the Most Dangerous Migratory Epidemic in the World"], UN News, March 17, 2020, https://news.un.org/es/story/2020/03/1471322; "Fears of Desert Locust Resurgence in Horn of Africa," UN News, November 24, 2020, https://news.un.org/en/story/2020/11/1078392.
10. Matt Simon, "The Terrible Consequences of Australia's Uber-Bushfires," *Wired*, July 20, 2020, https://www.wired.com/story/the-terrible-consequences-of-australias-uber-bushfires/.

will produce the greatest harvest of souls of all time. That final revival will empower the reapers—the remnant bride of Christ that God will send out from churches throughout the world—to reach the lost with signs, wonders, and miracles of all kinds. The new believers in Christ from that final harvest will be like the new wineskins into which new wine can be poured, which Jesus talked about in one of His parables in reference to the infilling of the Holy Spirit. (See, for example, Mark 2:22.) All that these believers do for the Lord will spring from a new filling with the Holy Spirit resulting from repentance and transformation. We will discuss this topic further in a coming chapter. When they go out and proclaim the gospel, they won't do it according to an intellectual approach. Instead, they will speak what the Spirit tells them to in each instance. The Lord has promised to do new things (see Revelation 21:5), things never before seen. And I'm sure He will!

These chaotic end times, which will be filled with unresolvable problems and crises, will lead many people to seek God. Their desperate search will bring about the final revival, with a glorious manifestation of God's Spirit.

Who will lead the people during the end-time revival? They will be led by the apostles and prophets of the remnant church. Apostles and prophets are custodians of the supernatural; therefore, they will be forerunners of the spiritual awakening in the last days. This is a major reason why the Holy Spirit has reestablished these two ministries during the last thirty or forty years, why He has restored honor and respect to these leadership roles. (See Ephesians 4:11–12.) He is empowering apostles and prophets for the task they must perform in the final days. Their assignment is to charge the spiritual atmosphere of the earth with God's glory and to awaken people's hearts to turn to God and enter into a supernatural lifestyle.

THE FATHERS OF EVERY MOVEMENT OF GOD HAVE ALWAYS BEEN THE APOSTLES AND PROPHETS.

Dear reader, as I emphasized earlier, there can be no effective revival without a shaking. The shaking will prepare the nations of the earth to receive the gospel. Unless people experience shaking, they are often unable to recognize the hand of God on earth or their need for Him. It is in the midst of crises that people seek refuge, comfort, and salvation in God. That is why, in this end-time cycle, we will continue to see shakings, followed by a revival that will ignite people's hearts, bringing millions to genuine repentance as they surrender their lives to the Lord Jesus.

I know people who, because of the shaking we are now experiencing—such as the coronavirus pandemic, financial crises, and so forth—have reconnected with the church through the Internet, simply by viewing online services. Before the shaking, they didn't want to hear from God; today, they have returned to the church because the signs reminded them of what is written in the Bible, and they know that there is no other way out besides God.

IF A NATION IS NOT SHAKEN OR BROKEN, IT WILL NOT HEAR THE GOSPEL.

AN URGENT MANDATE

After Jesus carries away His church in the rapture, the intense shaking of the great tribulation will come. During that time, people will still have a chance to receive salvation. However, being a Christian will cost many people their lives, because the Antichrist will be ruling over the earth, persecuting anyone who confesses the name of Jesus. (See, for example, Revelation 13:16–17.) Therefore, before the final shaking, the church must be dedicated to, and actively proclaiming, the crucified, risen, and victorious Christ. We must bring the gospel to a perplexed world desperate for solutions. Afterward, there will no longer be a church on earth that preaches the gospel because the bride of Christ will be in heaven with the Lord. "*Then I saw another angel flying in the midst of heaven, having the everlasting gospel to preach to those who dwell on the earth—to every nation, tribe, tongue, and people"* (Revelation 14:6).

THE SUPREME TASK OF THE CHURCH IS THE EVANGELIZATION OF THE WORLD.

The question is, are you telling others about the coming of the Lord while there is still time? Are you preaching the resurrection of Christ? Are you proclaiming the true gospel, or are you presenting mere motivational messages? The message of the coming of the Lord is what the enemy fears the most; therefore, in this time when the devil has risen up with all his weapons to block people from salvation and the supernatural, our message must be even more potent. It must include the power of Christ's resurrection, because when we preach about the King of Kings, the devil scatters.

THE PREACHING OF JESUS'S RETURN INSTILLS THE FEAR OF GOD IN PEOPLE AND LEADS THE CHURCH TO LIVE IN RIGHTEOUSNESS.

THE GLORY OF THE END TIMES

In the history of the church, we have seen the anointing of the Holy Spirit operating through men and women of God, particularly as they use their spiritual gifts. But we haven't consistently seen the glory of the Father sovereignly manifested, except in isolated cases where churches either are experiencing revival or have experienced revival. Yet, in these end times, we will witness sovereign acts of God. This will happen when we enter into His glory; and to do this, we must walk in the power of Christ's resurrection.

Sadly, in recent decades, the church has lost credibility and given a bad testimony to the world due to its religiosity, spiritual numbness, and lack of integrity. Because people do not trust the church anymore, God Himself will act sovereignly to demonstrate His power and mercy. Again,

His power will not be seen mainly through anointing (God using a person). Instead, God will sovereignly reveal Himself in a new realm of miracles; He will interrupt the normal course of events and break into the routine of church services to manifest His glory. People will stop looking to human beings for help and will have a supernatural, direct, and glorious experience with God the Father and His Son Jesus Christ. And it is the Holy Spirit who will lead us into God's presence.

As the true remnant of the church that seeks the Holy Spirit with hunger and passion for revival, we need to operate in our priestly anointing (see, for example, Revelation 1:6) and turn to prayer and fasting. We must come to know the person of the Holy Spirit so that He may lead us into the presence of the Father. Only then will we be the glorious church that Christ comes to seek. (See Ephesians 5:25–27.)

AT THE HEIGHT OF THE END-TIME REVIVAL, WE WILL SEE THE GLORY OF GOD.

I want to expand on this point because many believers have not fully understood it. Today, what we need even more than faith is the manifestation of God's glory. Jesus's resurrection from the dead did not require people's faith, because no one on earth had enough faith for it. Instead, He was raised to life *"by the glory of the Father"* (Romans 6:4). Jesus died bearing *all* the sins of mankind—from the beginning of human history to the end of time. The weight of carrying all that evil was horribly overwhelming, and the sentence of death for humanity's sin was irrevocable. But Jesus's victory over sin and death, and His subsequent explosive resurrection, became the portal through which power returned to the church. They are the source from which we can receive supernatural authority and provision today to proclaim the gospel of the kingdom with demonstrations of power, as the first apostles did: *"And with great power the apostles gave witness to the resurrection of the Lord Jesus. And great grace was upon them all"* (Acts 4:33).

Christ's resurrection is a spiritual portal through which the supernatural power of God flows into the church. This portal remains open where the resurrection continues to be preached and where God continues to manifest His power. In essence, every time we preach about the power of the resurrection, we exalt the glory of God and cause it to be manifest in our midst.

In these end times, we will see various spiritual portals open in the United States and around the world. Some will encompass entire regions; others will be limited to certain churches, families, or individuals. We will see various aspects of the Holy Spirit's power demonstrated in those regions, churches, and people, which will testify to what God is sovereignly saying and doing at that time. We will see portals of salvation, healing, wealth, personal transformation, miracles, signs, wonders, and the resurrection of the dead. All these supernatural works will bring spiritual revival. In other words, we will see an all-inclusive supernatural movement.

THE FINAL TESTIMONY WILL BE THE PREACHING OF THE GOSPEL WITH THE DEMONSTRATION OF THE POWER OF THE RESURRECTION IN THE NOW.

Therefore, in the final shaking—which, as I mentioned previously, will occur simultaneously with the revival—the glory of God will be revealed to the church. Jesus is coming back for a glorious church; this means that, in the midst of the shaking, the church will dwell in glory, revived by the Spirit of God! We will know that Jesus's appearance is imminent when we see the world continue to be shaken, the church enter into revival, and souls by the millions come to the feet of Christ in a great spiritual harvest.

THE FINAL SHAKING WILL LEAD PEOPLE TO RETURN TO PRAYER FOR REVIVAL.

THE COMING OF THE LORD

As for the manner in which the Lord will return, the Bible tells us that Jesus's appearing—the rapture—will occur first, followed later by His second coming. The Son of God will appear in order to take His bride, but He will come again to rule the earth during the millennium, and then to judge the world. *"I charge you therefore before God and the Lord Jesus Christ, who will judge the living and the dead at His appearing* [second coming] *and His kingdom"* (2 Timothy 4:1).

As we close chapter 1, I must emphasize that the remnant bride will be made up of those who have allowed God to process them during the shaking—those who have repented of their sins and spiritual slumber, humbled themselves before the Lord, and committed themselves fully to God, those who are continually seeking to be transformed by the Holy Spirit. I address this subject in depth in my book *Jesus Is Coming Soon*.

It is not wise to wait until the Lord takes His church in the rapture to begin seeking Him. *Today* is the day to seek God in fasting, prayer, worship, and obedience!

> Seek the LORD while He may be found, call upon Him while He is near. (Isaiah 55:6)

END-TIME TESTIMONIES

Joel is originally from California, USA, and he had been addicted to drugs and alcohol from the time he was a young teenager. A lack of identity and purpose in his life caused him to make many mistakes. However, he attended a revival conducted by King Jesus Ministry, and this led him to experience God at such a level that his life was totally transformed, to the point that he decided to move to Miami to be a part of our ministry.

I grew up in a loving home with my parents and four other siblings, but I felt alone and without identity. My father was an excellent provider, but he was an alcoholic. I drank my first beer at the age of twelve just to see why he drank. At thirteen, I became addicted to marijuana. After that, my life became a mess, and no one could help me. My parents tried everything to save me, but the more they tried, the more I rebelled. They even took me to a "healer" who subjected me to a horrible ritual.

When I was fifteen, I joined a gang. At seventeen, I met a girl, and, after three months, she became pregnant. That shocked me, but I married her because I wanted to be a good father to my baby. Unfortunately, we only lasted three months together. When I lost my family, I fell deeper into drugs and alcohol. I felt there was no way out for me!

Three years later, by some miracle, I returned to live with my wife, since we had never officially divorced. I knew that our restoration had begun. We started attending a church in California, where I gave my life to Christ. I believed that my problems would disappear as if by magic, but, instead, a terrible spiritual struggle began. One night, after my wife came home from work, we began to argue. The argument escalated into a physical fight, and I ended up in jail for domestic violence. My wife was determined to divorce me, but then she learned that she was expecting our second child. When I was released from jail after three weeks, she decided to stay with me.

A few months later, our pastors gave us tickets to a King Jesus Ministry conference in Miami. I had never been to a conference before, and I had great expectations! I wanted change! That week in Miami, I experienced God's presence like never before, and the spiritual revival transformed me. There, we discovered that God had a purpose for our lives. When we returned to California, we began following King Jesus meetings on YouTube, and we grew spiritually. Then, God performed a financial miracle, enabling us to move to Miami. Today, we live in the midst of the revival at King Jesus Ministry, serving the Lord. I was freed from all addictions, and our marriage was restored. We have also been blessed with a business of our own. Now, we are part of this great supernatural movement, and I thank God for all His blessings.

Jose Ramon from the United States began to believe God for a creative miracle when his wife was unable to conceive. In 2016, after Jose made a covenant with God, his wife became pregnant. Yet in the midst of their joy over this miracle, the baby was diagnosed with Down syndrome. About that time, our ministry was hosting its annual Apostolic and Prophetic Conference (CAP), and during this event, there is always a very powerful spiritual movement. Jose explains how they received a miracle:

> We wanted to have children but weren't able to. During the Apostolic and Prophetic Conference (CAP) in 2016, we made a covenant with God to have a baby, and He did the miracle! Within a year, my wife became pregnant. However, at six months, the doctor told us that there was an 80 percent chance the child would have Down syndrome. We continued to pray and believe for what God had promised in that covenant. The doctor scheduled an appointment with us that coincided with the dates of CAP 2017. He told us that we had two options: to keep the baby or abort it. If we kept it, we would have to take classes to learn how to care for it.
>
> We decided to have our baby, knowing that God would fulfill His promise. We left the appointment and attended the CAP event, asking the Lord to heal our baby. In particular, I asked the Lord for a confirmation. During the last session, while the manifest presence of God was ministering to our hearts, a boy of about twelve years of age came up to me, hugged me, and said, "Don't worry." That message was wonderful and so encouraging! After three weeks, my wife had another checkup, and, to the glory of God, the doctor confirmed that everything was fine. The child was healthy! He was developing normally! Today, we give all the glory to God for what He did and for His faithfulness. Although we had tribulations, He was faithful to His promise, and we received our breakthrough at CAP. He has brought revival in so many areas of our lives, and now we can enjoy His promises fulfilled.

PART I:

GOD IS SHAKING THE EARTH

CHAPTER 2

THE END-TIME SHAKING

The times in which we are living mark the beginning of the end of an era—the era of the Holy Spirit (also called the age of the church), which will conclude when Jesus appears at the rapture. The close of an era signifies the completion of one aspect of God's purposes, signaling the end of something old and the birth of something new, whereas *the fullness of the times* (Ephesians 1:10), which we discussed in the previous chapter, signifies the completion of *all* things. *"The fullness of the times"* will be the climax of times and seasons, and the consummation of life in this present world. That is the point when God will *"gather together in one all things in Christ, both which are in heaven and which are on earth—in Him"* (Ephesians 1:10). Again, the events that will signify the fullness of the times are the second coming of Christ, His millennial reign, and the last judgment.

SIGNS AND SEASONS

Every season in life is identified by certain signs. In the natural world, in the northern hemisphere, autumn is generally marked by the falling of leaves from the trees, winter by lower temperatures and snowfall, spring by the blossoming of flowers, and summer by higher temperatures and the growth of vegetation. Today, we are in a supernatural season of shaking, and we must be prepared to see spiritual and physical signs of it. Not only was this season prophesied in the Old Testament, but Jesus spoke of it as well.

(See, for example, Haggai 2:6–7; Matthew 24:5–8.) Signs of this season—such as tsunamis, floods, fires, hurricanes, and more—have already been manifesting in our physical world. CNN presented a detailed assessment of hurricanes suffered by the United States and the Caribbean islands over the last thirty years.[11] There has been an increase in the number of intense hurricanes, with sustained intensity after landfall, and that trend will continue.[12] We are also seeing pestilences, diseases, epidemics, perplexities, civil wars, anarchy, and people flooding the streets demanding their rights. We are living in days of great upheaval. Researchers and analysts may be able to describe events that are happening and to provide some scientific and societal explanations for them, but they usually do so from a human perspective alone. As believers, we are not to just focus on the earthly manifestations but to discern the spiritual meaning behind them and respond accordingly.

For example, as we talked about in the previous chapter, the world has been dealing with the plague of the coronavirus, or COVID-19. The nature of the virus's origin is still being debated, and it has proven to be very difficult to contain, with variants emerging and causing new surges of sickness and death. At the beginning of 2021, many people in the United States were waiting in long lines, desperately seeking to receive their first dose of a vaccine. Millions around the world still did not have access to vaccines. As 2021 progressed, numbers of people chose not to be vaccinated, others were still unable to obtain vaccines, and coronavirus cases with the Delta variant surged worldwide. There have even been some "breakthrough" infections in which vaccinated people have contracted the virus. As I write this book, there are still many questions about when this plague will end.

I believe it will stop when its purpose is concluded. God is not the author of disease or sickness, but from a spiritual point of view, this virus is one sign that a new end-time season has begun; it points to the prophesied

---

11. "Notable Hurricanes in Recent US History," Hurricane Statistics Fast Facts, CNN, July 8, 2021, https://edition.cnn.com/2013/05/31/world/americas/hurricane-statistics-fast-facts/index.html.

12. Doyle Rice, "Are Category 5 Hurricanes Such as Dorian the 'New Normal'?" *USA Today*, September 11, 2019, https://www.usatoday.com/story/news/nation/2019/09/11/category-5-hurricanes-storms-like-dorian-new-normal/2275423001/; Matt McGrath, "Climate Change: Hurricanes Get Stronger on Land as World Warms," BBC News, November 11, 2020, https://www.bbc.com/news/science-environment-54902068.

last days as well as to Jesus's return. There has been movement in the spiritual dimension, and what we see manifested on earth is a consequence of what is happening in the spiritual world.

THE NATURAL REALM AND THE SPIRITUAL REALM

Everything related to human beings and what they do is connected to the spiritual realm. However, most people cannot easily explain the spiritual dimension because they do not understand it. They do not fully know themselves or the Bible, much less comprehend what is happening around them and why. They are unaware of the spiritual realm that surrounds and influences them. Again, human beings can only monitor and explain, to a certain extent, the natural elements they grasp through their physical senses. They cannot see or understand the spiritual dimension without the help of God's Holy Spirit. *"The natural man does not receive the things of the Spirit of God, for they are foolishness to him; nor can he know them, because they are spiritually discerned"* (1 Corinthians 2:14).

IF WE DO NOT RETURN TO THE DIMENSION OF THE SPIRIT, WE WILL NOT UNDERSTAND GOD AND HIS PURPOSES.

If we were to remove the spiritual realm, there would be no universe and no humankind because the natural dimension depends on the spiritual for its existence.

In the beginning God created the heavens and the earth.
(Genesis 1:1)

By the word of the LORD the heavens were made, and all the host of them by the breath of His mouth. (Psalm 33:6)

So God created man in His own image; in the image of God He created him; male and female He created them. (Genesis 1:27)

Moreover, the spiritual realm governs the natural; therefore, nothing that is happening in the world right now—whether environmentally, politically, economically, physically, or emotionally—is outside of spiritual influence. Everything has a spiritual background, cause, and meaning.

I am not referring only to the heavenly spiritual realm and its influence but also to the demonic realm and its influence, which are in opposition to God and which will be completely removed in the fullness of the times. For example, studies by "the World Health Organization (WHO) and the *Global Burden of Disease...*estimate that almost 800,000 people die from suicide every year. That's one person every 40 seconds."[13] Older people are the most affected age group, and men are twice as likely as women to end their own lives.[14] Other studies reveal that most of the world's population lives in poverty. Two-thirds live on less than ten dollars a day, and one in ten lives on less than two dollars a day, which is what the World Bank of the United Nations considers "extreme poverty."[15] While, outwardly, these dire conditions might seem to be caused by various social, economic, and physical factors, those who are in tune with the supernatural realm can see that there is a spiritual dimension to them as well—the enemy is using spirits of suicide and poverty to torment people around the world.

Once more, God's Holy Spirit is the only One who fully knows what is happening in our world and why. He knows the times and seasons in God's plan for humanity, this planet, and the universe. The good news is that the Spirit still speaks—both through the Scriptures and directly—to God's people, those who believe in Jesus Christ and obey Him.

Before leaving this earth and ascending to heaven, Jesus told His disciples, *"However, when He, the Spirit of truth, has come, He will guide you into all truth; for He will not speak on His own authority, but whatever He hears He will speak; and He will tell you things to come"* (John 16:13). The Holy Spirit can give you a spiritual perspective to understand what is happening behind the scenes in the world today; you will be able to recognize the season in the spiritual realm that is currently being reflected by what

---

13. Hannah Ritchie, Max Roser, and Esteban Ortiz-Ospina, "Suicide," Our World in Data, 2015, https://ourworldindata.org/suicide.

14. Ritchie, Roser, and Ortiz-Ospina, "Suicide."

15. Max Roser and Esteban Ortiz-Ospina, "Global Extreme Poverty," Our World in Data, 2019, https://ourworldindata.org/extreme-poverty.

is going on in the natural world. As you do, you will be able to comprehend what has not previously made sense to you about the shaking we are experiencing.

The Spirit is using God's apostles and prophets to call the church's attention to this supernatural season and to prepare us to be His remnant in these last days. However, there is still much confusion among people in the church because many preachers are essentially rejecting the Holy Spirit and His power at a time when it is vital to have His revelation and counsel. Their resulting blindness and deafness to the Spirit prevents them from comprehending why the world is so shaken, which keeps them from passing along the revelation to their congregations. They lack knowledge—and, above all, wisdom—to lead people during these times. Instead, they further confuse those who listen to them. They cannot provide revelation-filled answers to the questions people ask; neither do they know how to personally face these days or prepare for what is coming.

IT IS IMPOSSIBLE TO KNOW THE WILL OF GOD IF WE ARE NOT LED BY THE HOLY SPIRIT.

WHAT IS BEHIND THE SHAKING?

For thus says the LORD of hosts: "Once more (it is a little while) I will shake heaven and earth, the sea and dry land; and I will shake all nations, and they shall come to the Desire of All Nations."
(Haggai 2:6–7)

[God's] *voice then* [when He gave the law on Mount Sinai] *shook the earth; but now He has promised, saying, "Yet once more I shake not only the earth, but also heaven." Now this, "Yet once more," indicates the removal of those things that are being shaken, as of things that are made, that the things which cannot be shaken may remain.*
(Hebrews 12:26–27)

In these passages, God is saying, "I will shake heaven and earth!" Although Satan and human beings cause oppression, pain, and death in the world, it is not ultimately the devil or men who are behind the end-time shaking, but rather God Himself. He is the only One who can create a global shaking such as we are experiencing. Therefore, the shaking is not something we can pray against. Instead, we must go through it because it is a sign of the end time that is taking place as a sovereign act of God.

In Haggai 2:6–7, the Hebrew word for *"shake"* is *rā'ash*, among whose meanings are "to undulate (as the earth, the sky, etc.; also a field of grain), particularly through fear," "to make afraid," "to make to shake," and "to make to tremble." When the Bible speaks of shaking in this way, it refers to an awesome demonstration of God's power.

The above verses from Hebrews 12 explain how, on Mount Sinai, when God gave the tablets of the law to Moses to be obeyed by the people of Israel, He shook the earth. This event is considered to be the first Pentecost. The second Pentecost occurred when the Holy Spirit descended upon the one hundred and twenty disciples of Jesus who were praying and waiting for His promise in the upper room. At that time, the earth again shook. (See Acts 4:31.) Today, God is shaking the earth once more, this time on a global scale.

This shaking has three stages to it: a preliminary stage, which we went through at the beginning of the twenty-first century with the consecutive terrorist attacks; an intermediate stage (the stage we are in now); and a final stage (which was actually initiated with the arrival of the decade of the 2020s but will grow increasingly intense). Again, the final stage will lead to the culmination of the Holy Spirit's season on earth, which will be characterized by unprecedented spiritual revival and harvest. We are on the cusp of the zero hour appointed for the earth before Christ's appearing. We are the generation that is seeing the greatest fulfillment of biblical prophecies, and, without a doubt, we will see the return of the Lord.

THE ULTIMATE SIGN OF CHRIST'S APPEARING IS THE GLOBAL SHAKING.

During times of divine shaking, sovereign acts of God will challenge human knowledge.

And there will be signs in the sun, in the moon, and in the stars; and on the earth distress of nations, with perplexity, the sea and the waves roaring; men's hearts failing them from fear and the expectation of those things which are coming on the earth, for the powers of the heavens will be shaken. (Luke 21:25–26)

"The sun, the moon, and the stars" can represent human beings' range of understanding, their capacity to see and comprehend the world in which they live. They signify the light of human education, wisdom, and knowledge acquired over the centuries. We know that such knowledge is limited, and the limitations of human ability are being exposed in the end-time shaking. When people experience shakings, they become disoriented, distracted, confused, anxious, worried, and afraid. This happens because things that seemed to be secure in their lives and environment are being displaced and removed. The troubling times we are living in are leaving people perplexed, in crisis, feeling as if there is no way out. They have no appropriate answers because everything they know is being shaken. Their earthly knowledge is insufficient to provide real, sustainable solutions to today's crises. When people are unable to understand, explain, or interpret what is happening in the world, this leads them to cry out to God for wisdom and help.

THE BASIS OF OUR TRUST IN GOD IS THAT HE KNOWS THE FINAL OUTCOME.

For example, the world economy is being shaken as a divine sign for man to repent and seek God. That is why we have experienced financial crises like the stock market crash of 2008 and other economic troubles. God is demonstrating that He is the true owner of all the silver and gold in the world. We must realize that the purpose of these signs is to capture humanity's attention because God knows that it is during such crises that people turn to Him. He has the answers through the Holy Spirit for those who seek Him from their hearts.

As I described earlier, it is not only the world economy that is being shaken and will continue to be shaken. We have seen a shaking in our weather patterns. Nature is confused, and, consequently, so is our climate. God is systematically shaking *all* things. Nations, governments, political systems, educational institutions, commerce, religious denominations, churches, ministries, families, relationships, physical structures, mountains and other natural elements, times and seasons, and the devil himself are being shaken. The only Person who is not being shaken, and for whom the purpose of the shaking is clear, is the One who is producing it. From God's perspective, this apparently chaotic shaking is bringing order because it is in accord with His plan for the end times.

In these times, evangelism becomes key as people search for true security. People need someone to help them find salvation in Christ and receive the indwelling Holy Spirit. Therefore, during the shaking, we must preach the gospel with boldness, with a demonstration of God's power, and in a personal way, as Jesus did with the woman at the well. (See John 4:1–42.) The most powerful testimony is that which results from a personal experience with the power of God. That is irrefutable!

FOUNDED EITHER ON ROCK OR SAND

Nothing that can be shaken will remain unshaken. Every dimension or sphere of life that is not grounded in God will fall away, while anything that is established in Him will remain. (See Hebrews 12:27.) This is what Jesus explained in the parable of the two foundations, or the parable of the wise and foolish builders:

> But why do you call Me "Lord, Lord," and not do the things which I say? Whoever comes to Me, and hears My sayings and does them, I will show you whom he is like: He is like a man building a house, who dug deep and laid the foundation on the rock. And when the flood arose, the stream beat vehemently against that house, and could not shake it, for it was founded on the rock. But he who heard and did

nothing is like a man who built a house on the earth without a founda-
tion, against which the stream beat vehemently; and immediately it fell.
And the ruin of that house was great. (Luke 6:46–49)

Is your life built on sand? Or is it built on rock? Is your faith based only on the things you can see, or is it established on the eternal God? If your faith is in material things, it will definitely be shaken. Anyone can claim to have faith. But when a crisis comes, and they are shaken, the foundation on which their faith is founded will be revealed. Our faith must be established on Christ, the firm Rock. (See, for example, Acts 4:10–12.)

WHEN GOD SHAKES A HOUSE, THE FOUNDATION ON WHICH IT IS BUILT IS REVEALED.

No matter who you are or what you do, you will not escape this end-time shaking. We will all have to go through it. The only difference will be that if our foundation is built on Christ, we will stand firm and have answers for these times of crisis; but if our foundation is built on something material, temporal, or spiritually weak, we will be shaken until we wholeheartedly seek God.

No matter what happens on earth, God will not change. (See, for example, James 1:17.) He cannot be moved or shaken. (See, for example, Psalm 62:2.) He is in full control. We must rest in this knowledge as we experience shaking in our lives, knowing that if we remain in Christ, we will stand fast. Hebrews 12:28 says, *"Therefore, since we are receiving a king-dom which cannot be shaken, let us have grace, by which we may serve God acceptably with reverence and godly fear."*

FOUR ASPECTS OF THE END-TIME SHAKING

We must understand that there are four aspects to the end-time shaking: (1) judgment of the house of God, or the church; (2) judgment of the nations; (3) the shaking of all nations; and (4) the revelation of God's glory.

1. JUDGMENT OF THE HOUSE OF GOD

In the Scriptures, we read that judgment starts with God's people:

For the time has come for judgment to begin at the house of God; and if it begins with us first, what will be the end of those who do not obey the gospel of God? (1 Peter 4:17)

But in accordance with your hardness and your impenitent heart you are treasuring up for yourself wrath in the day of wrath and revelation of the righteous judgment of God, who "will render to each one according to his deeds." (Romans 2:5–6)

God loves His people; therefore, because He knows the end is coming, He is judging the apostate church—that portion of the church, especially its leaders, that panders to people's fleshly desires, believing that in this way they will keep their congregations stable, instead of leading people to repent of their sins. Both the apostate church and the remnant bride will be revealed in the end times. The latter is the church within the church, which keeps "watching and praying" (see, for example, Mark 13:33), and which is distinguished by the supernatural, holiness, and a hunger for God.

THE MOST DISTINCTIVE MARK OF THE REMNANT IS THE SUPERNATURAL.

If you are a leader in your church, and you are a people pleaser, then beware: this is not the time to be indulging the world. You need to repent and seek God because you will be shaken. Christ's remnant must have the ability to meet people's needs with the supernatural power of God. This is not possible by conforming to what the people want done but only by doing what God wants done. The survival of the church in the days to come will depend on our walking in divine supernatural power; otherwise, we will become irrelevant. We will have no real answers for the crucial needs of individuals, communities, and nations.

Regardless of whether a particular shaking is intended for the remnant, that shaking will reveal God's true and faithful followers, for God will preserve His remnant amid the outpouring of His wrath. Thus, Isaiah announced, *"Come, my people, enter your chambers, and shut your doors behind you; hide yourself, as it were, for a little moment, until the indignation is past"* (Isaiah 26:20). What we do, what we create, and how we act in a time of God's shaking will reveal our identity in God, our authenticity, our spiritual knowledge, and our position in Christ. If we are the remnant church, God will sustain us.

THE FIRST SHAKING STARTS WITH THE HOUSE OF GOD BECAUSE NOT EVERYONE IN IT IS PART OF THE REMNANT.

2. JUDGMENT OF THE NATIONS

Another aspect of end-time shaking is God's judgment of the nations. The Bible speaks about God having cups or vessels in which various things accumulate—such as His salvation, His mercy, the prayers of His people, His wrath, and the iniquity of mankind. (See, for example, Revelation 5:8; 16:19.) When the capacity of a cup is reached, or when God so commands, that cup is poured out upon the earth. At this moment, two cups are overflowing: the cup of God's wrath—because of man's iniquity or wickedness—and the cup of His mercy. These cups hold centuries' worth of accumulation and have reached their fullness. God will judge those who have sown iniquity and bless those who have sown mercy.

The shaking is God's indignant scourging of humanity, which, in complete rebellion, lives without faith, without God, and without hope in the world (see Ephesians 2:12), despising the life and creation that God has entrusted to it. Thus, the prophet Isaiah anticipated, *"For behold, the LORD comes out of His place to punish the inhabitants of the earth for their iniquity; the earth will also disclose her blood, and will no more cover her slain"* (Isaiah 26:21).

As I explained in chapter 1, the shaking of the church is different from the shaking of the world. The shaking of the world is for judgment, while the shaking of the church is for purification. All the plagues that God sent to Egypt were aimed at its government, but God protected His people, and He preserved their firstborn from death through the blood of the sacrificial lamb. (See, for example, Exodus 12:13.) Similarly, you must apply the blood of Jesus to your life in order to be spiritually saved and preserved. (See, for example, 1 John 1:7; Revelation 1:5.)

3. THE SHAKING OF ALL NATIONS

"And I will shake all nations" (Haggai 2:7). In chapter 1, I wrote that the last-days shaking is a sign to the church, Israel, and the world that we are in the end times. Again, when we see the coronavirus shaking the whole world, we must recognize it as a sign of the last days. Whether the virus was man-made or animal-borne, God allowed it, as He will allow future plagues that will ravage the earth as end-time signs.

In these last days, God is shaking all nations to prepare them for the witnesses from the remnant church who will preach the gospel to them. As I have been emphasizing, if people are not shaken or broken, they will not be open to hearing the gospel. The shaking brings judgment and mercy at the same time—judgment for the unrepentant and mercy for those who humble themselves and submit their lives to God.

THE SHAKING COMES TO JUDGE, REBUKE, AND CORRECT, BUT REPENTANCE CAUSES GOD TO DELAY OR STOP HIS JUDGMENT.

---

4. THE REVELATION OF GOD'S GLORY

The earth is about to conclude the cycle that began with the glory of God and will end with that same glory. The prophet Isaiah announced this when he said:

Arise, shine; for your light has come! And the glory of the LORD is risen upon you. For behold, the darkness shall cover the earth, and deep darkness the people; but the LORD will arise over you, and His glory will be seen upon you. The Gentiles shall come to your light, and kings to the brightness of your rising. (Isaiah 60:1–3)

Again, the church has an appointment with a tremendous outpouring of the Holy Spirit—the end-time revival and harvest. We are about to experience an unprecedented awakening among the children of God; it will be something the earth has never seen before, and it will happen in the midst of the greatest shaking the world has ever experienced. The shaking in the church will bring an outpouring of God's glory, which will prepare the remnant for the rapture, because Jesus is returning for a glorious church. (See Ephesians 5:26–27.) The church will be in glory in the midst of the shaking, so, while the world is in chaos, the church will be seen as a place of refuge.

THOSE WHO HAVE NO KNOWLEDGE OF THE GLORY WILL ONLY DRAW JUDGMENT.

WHICH OUTPOURING WILL YOU RECEIVE?

Let me ask you again, whose side are you on? From which outpouring are you ready to receive: the cup of judgment or the cup of mercy? Will you experience the curse or the blessing? This is the time to face the truth about your faith and how you have lived it up to today. The shaking comes to the children of God to awaken them out of the deep sleep of convenience and comfort. Following Christ is not easy. After all, He did not promise an easy path but quite the contrary. (See, for example, Matthew 16:24–25.) To follow Him, we must die to the desires of the flesh, to the pleasures of this world, to the pride of life, and to success as the world defines it. (See, for example, 1 John 2:16.) We must die to live, and we must lose to gain. (See, for example, John 12:24.) Believers must begin to remember these truths, seeking God with all their hearts, and take their places as members of the remnant church—as the glorious bride that will manifest the power of God on earth and prepare the way for the coming of Jesus Christ.

END-TIME TESTIMONIES

Mario Davila attends King Jesus Ministry in Miami. During the COVID-19 epidemic, his uncle in Nicaragua, who was in his early sixties, was exposed to the virus, and the doctors gave him two weeks to live. When his body was no longer functioning, Mario and his wife, who are filled with the Holy Spirit, called upon God.

My wife and I have been able to witness the hand of God during this recent crisis. Our faith has been ignited by the miracles we have seen in our families. My wife's uncle and his coworkers contracted the coronavirus. However, even though this uncle's coworkers were dying, he went through the disease without experiencing any symptoms.

In addition, my sixty-one-year-old uncle contracted the coronavirus and spent a month in the hospital, being intubated for sixteen days. He was experiencing kidney failure, liver failure, heart failure, and lung failure. The doctors informed his son that he had only a 10 percent chance of living. They told him that there was nothing to be done, that his father would die within two weeks. My family created an Internet family chat room to find out how my uncle's brothers were going to deal with this situation. They expected the worst. In fact, some of my family members were praying that God's will would be done by accepting the possibility of his death. However, I told them, "No! We're going to believe that Christ is going to revive him and that he's going to serve God." Miraculously, my uncle recovered. Of the six patients who were with him, only two survived, a young man and my uncle. It was a miracle! We were able to see God's power manifested, a visible before-and-after for His glory. Now, I can testify that my family is living in great revival and that God used this process to show us His love.

The following is the testimony of a woman who, amid a shaking world, surrendered her life to God and now lives in the supernatural, from miracle to miracle. While others despair trying to find a way out of impossible problems, she turns to God and sees the impossible happen.

My name is Edenia, and I am originally from Cuba. I converted to the Lord in 2014. I was a victim of domestic violence, and I had a four-year-old girl and no resources. When I immigrated to the United States, I arrived full of fears. During my childhood, my parents were not bad people, but they divorced, and their separation marked my heart with resentment. But after I went to my first retreat at King Jesus Ministry, the Lord began to remove unforgiveness, resentment, and fear from me. Then, everything began to fall into place. What impacted me the most was feeling clean for the first time. The Lord forgave all of my past.

I had been attending King Jesus Ministry for no more than a year when I had an experience that impacted me further. One day, at church, I was very impressed by the spiritual atmosphere; I had an encounter with the Lord in which I dared to believe in His provision and made a covenant with Him concerning the remaining money in my bank account—just ten dollars—to buy a house, and God was faithful. I asked the Lord for a two-story, three-bedroom, two-and-a-half-bath house. I desired to be a House of Peace[16] leader, so I wanted a spacious corner house with a bathroom on the first floor. I had included so much detail in my prayer request that my family thought I was asking for too much. But in August 2015, I received exactly the house I had asked for. Now, I dare to believe God for anything.

That same year, I started to petition God on behalf of my half-sister, her husband, and their son to join me in the United States. People told me it would be impossible for them to be approved by immigration, but I believed God. When I went to CAP 2015, I made a covenant and believed that before Mother's Day 2016, my sister and her family would be in the United States. Normally, the process takes two to five years; however, they arrived in the country the Sunday before Mother's Day 2016, just as I'd declared it. That same year, I lost my job, but not my faith. Again, I made a

---

16. A House of Peace refers to the home of a member of King Jesus International Ministry or its associate churches who welcomes neighbors, relatives, and friends for the purpose of sharing the gospel of the kingdom—teaching the Word of God and imparting His power. The same anointing, supernatural power, and presence of God that are found in the main King Jesus Ministry church manifest there.

covenant with God, saying, "Lord, I don't want a little job. I want a real job in my profession, with benefits." And the Lord was good because, that same year, I started working for the government with vacation pay, a retirement plan, and health insurance. I've already had five promotions!

In 2017, I was diagnosed with a cyst of about four centimeters near my left ovary. I could even feel it from the outside. When the doctor wanted to schedule surgery, I told him no, I believed in a supernatural God, and the scalpel was not going to touch my body. In a church meeting, a prophet prayed for women with cysts and declared healing. At that moment, I felt the cyst was gone. After three weeks, I went to the doctor because he said he could not postpone the surgery any longer. When I told him I didn't have the cyst anymore, he smiled in disbelief. He did two ultrasounds because he could not find the cyst in the first one. Finally, he said to me, "It's true; it does not exist. Have you not had any pain? Have you not felt anything?" I answered, "No, I have only felt the glory of God in my life, and I know that He healed me."

At CAP 2018, I dared to believe the Lord for my debts; I told Him that I wanted to enter 2019 debt free. So, I made a covenant and believed. I had a beautiful encounter with the Lord, and my faith grew. I made a covenant to refinance my house and pay off my debts. In 2019, I started the process, and today I can testify that I refinanced all the debt and the house. I received a call from the bank offering me a virtually unheard-of interest rate, even for people with good credit. I stopped paying over $40,000 in interest. My debt was paid off in full!

CHAPTER 3

THE MORAL CORRUPTION OF MANKIND

The moral corruption of mankind began with humanity's rebellion against God in the garden of Eden. (See Genesis 3.) Since that time, human beings' internal corruption has affected every aspect of their relationships with God and other people. And, through the millennia, it has also negatively influenced every segment of society: government, politics, business, religion, the arts, sports, music, science, health, and more. Although each generation has manifested the effects of moral degeneration due to sin, the Bible tells us that the influence and manifestation of this depravity will grow dramatically in the end times. People's hearts will become increasingly corrupt. And in the first portion of the twenty-first century, we have only seen an increase in the degradation of human character.

In the natural world, we know that when an apple has begun to rot, nothing can stop its complete decomposition or prevent it from spoiling all the other fruit around it. Corruption works the same way no matter where we find it. Apart from salvation in Christ, moral corruption is irreversible in the human race. That is why no one on earth has an effective plan to stop it—not governments, institutions, or organized religion. Only God knows how to deal with it, and it is not by improving man, or even by restoring him, but by making him *brand-new in Christ*. That is why Jesus told Nicodemus, *"Most assuredly, I say to you, unless one is **born again**, he cannot see the kingdom of God"* (John 3:3).

Regeneration in Jesus is the answer to mankind's moral corruption, but human beings have persistently refused to surrender to God and His plans for humanity. Paul specifically warned Timothy that *"in the last days perilous times will come"* (2 Timothy 3:1). The term *"perilous times"* indicates dangerous, violent, stressful times, influenced by great demonic activity. *"For we do not wrestle against flesh and blood, but against principalities, against powers, against the rulers of the darkness of this age, against spiritual hosts of wickedness in the heavenly places"* (Ephesians 6:12). I believe that, today, we are living in those dangerous times where demonic influence abounds, not only through violence, but also through immorality. That demonic influence has come upon many people, and, as a result, we are seeing the moral corruption that the apostle Paul declared would be characteristic of the end times:

> But know this, that in the last days perilous times will come: for men will be lovers of themselves, lovers of money, boasters, proud, blasphemers, disobedient to parents, unthankful, unholy, unloving, unforgiving, slanderers, without self-control, brutal, despisers of good, traitors, headstrong, haughty, lovers of pleasure rather than lovers of God, having a form of godliness but denying its power. And from such people turn away! For of this sort are those who creep into households and make captives of gullible women loaded down with sins, led away by various lusts, always learning and never able to come to the knowledge of the truth. Now as Jannes and Jambres resisted Moses, so do these also resist the truth: men of corrupt minds, disapproved concerning the faith.   (2 Timothy 3:1–8)

Jesus announced that the last days would be like the days of Noah:

> Then the Lord saw that the wickedness of man was great in the earth, and that every intent of the thoughts of his heart was only evil continually. And the Lord was sorry that He had made man on the earth, and He was grieved in His heart.... The earth also was corrupt before God, and the earth was filled with violence. So God looked upon the earth, and indeed it was corrupt; for all flesh had corrupted their way on the earth. And God said to Noah, "The end of all flesh has come before

Me, for the earth is filled with violence through them; and behold, I will destroy them with the earth." (Genesis 6:5–6, 11–13)

But as the days of Noah were, so also will the coming of the Son of Man be. For as in the days before the flood, they were eating and drinking, marrying and giving in marriage, until the day that Noah entered the ark, and did not know until the flood came and took them all away, so also will the coming of the Son of Man be. (Matthew 24:37–39)

Noah's generation was marked by hardness of heart and deafness to the voice of God. At that time, the wickedness of human beings was great, with all their thoughts being evil. The earth was filled with violence, and all flesh was corrupt. Therefore, the Lord brought judgment upon the earth through the flood, destroying all human life except for Noah and his family. Mankind's moral condition is the same today as it was then. The end-time shaking our world is experiencing testifies to the corruption of human beings and their refusal to hear the voice of God. Demonic activity is at its peak now, and there is no turning back.

THE MORAL CORRUPTION OF MAN IS THE MAIN CAUSE OF THE SHAKING BECAUSE IT BRINGS GOD'S JUDGMENT.

WHAT IS MORALITY?

To better understand what the moral corruption of mankind refers to, I would first like to establish what morals are. A person's morals are their beliefs regarding what is acceptable and unacceptable in their life and in society. It indicates their code of conduct or standard of behavior. Individuals, families, people groups, and nations are sustained by holding righteous values and practicing them. Widespread positive morality among people is a condition for establishing and maintaining a righteous and just society. When God established Israel as a people and a nation, the first thing He gave them was a moral code because that is the lining of the fabric of society; it is what instructs and forms the character of its members.

Let's explore this idea further. God created all nations but chose the nation of Israel to be different, separate from the rest, as a reflection His own nature. *"Righteousness and justice are the foundation of Your throne; mercy and truth go before Your face"* (Psalm 89:14). The Israelites' approach to life was to be different, especially from a moral point of view. God gave them certain laws and codes of conduct, which were so sound and wholesome in nature that many are still maintained today, especially among Christian societies around the world. The basis for these laws was the Ten Commandments (see Exodus 20:1–17), whose influence has even reached the legal sphere of our time. For example, in today's world, there are laws against murder, bearing false witness, stealing, and so forth, all of which are drawn from the Israelite moral code.

A PERSON'S MORALITY SHAPES THEIR CHARACTER.

Today, we see that positive moral values in the family and in society are increasingly being watered down and disappearing. When such values diminish in a society, that society becomes corrupt and is eventually destroyed. The nation of the United States, for example, was born and founded upon the biblical moral principles that God gave to the people of Israel. But nowadays, we have strayed from that foundation so much that we need to ask, "Is the US still a Christian nation, or is it simply a nation with a number of Christians in it?" The evidence of a nation submitted to God is justice and righteous judgment. How can we say that we are a nation that is submitted to God, with Christian morals, when our land lacks justice? We see people suffering physical harm at the hands of others, the blood of the innocent being shed, leaders abusing their power and oppressing the weak, the rich exploiting the poor, and other forms of unrighteousness.

God's values are expressed in the Bible, and they begin with these clear principles:

You shall love the LORD *your God with all your heart, with all your soul, and with all your strength.*   (Deuteronomy 6:5)

You shall fear [strongly reverence with awe] *the* LORD *your God; you shall serve Him, and to Him you shall hold fast, and take oaths in His name.*   (Deuteronomy 10:20)

All the values found in the Ten Commandments are based upon these principles. Today, there are many people who do not love or fear God and likewise do not teach their children to love, fear, serve, and follow Him. For this reason, righteous moral values are being lost. If we lack these foundational principles, we have no basis for developing societal values that proceed from them.

After a commitment to following God and His ways, a commitment to building a loving, strong, and unified family in the Lord is the most fundamental moral value a person can have. God created man and woman and gave them the mandate to *"be fruitful and multiply"* (Genesis 1:28); therefore, marriage is a divine institution, and marriage was, is, and must always be between a man and a woman. When we remove these basic values related to the family, we create dysfunctional families.

Today, there is a growing lack of fathers in the home due to marital separation and divorce, as well as to men abandoning their families after having children with their partners outside of marriage. In God's plan, men are to serve as the priests of their families. (See, for example, 1 Corinthians 11:3.) When men are absent from the family, women are forced to assume the role of spiritual leader, as well as to fulfill their own roles. Additionally, children grow up without fathers to guide them and consequently lack a real sense of identity. This is currently the case in our society. Today, we can say that we live on a planet of orphans because this generation is full of children who lack identity, and of prodigal sons and daughters who turn to drugs, sexual immorality, and other vices because they have not grown up in a loving home that is based on God's values.

In another example of lost values, American society, for the most part, accepts abortion as normal. It considers abortion to be "a woman's right to control her own body," regardless of the rights of the person in her womb.[17] In the US, the acceptance of abortion has generally increased over the last sixty years because the nation has lost the moral values of the Creator. But no matter what society thinks, abortion continues to be a sin before God that separates us from Him and yields terrible consequences. The value of life has been lost! Today, animals are often valued more than a baby in its mother's womb.

In our society, sin is constantly being legalized. Everyone is selfishly defending their own rights, but relatively few are defending God's causes— the rights of those of the innocent, the rights of those who cannot defend themselves. (See, for example, James 1:27.) As Christians, we must stand up for lost moral values such as justice, integrity, truth, righteousness, and mercy. *"If the foundations are destroyed, what can the righteous do?"* (Psalm 11:3).

WHAT IS CORRUPTION?

Now that we have defined morality, let us explore the definition of corruption. The word *corruption* simply means perversion, decay, rottenness, and ruin. In the moral realm, corruption refers to "dishonest or illegal behavior especially by powerful people," "inducement to wrong by improper or unlawful means (such as bribery)," "a departure from the original or from what is pure or correct," and "immoral conduct or practices harmful or offensive to society."[18] Included in these definitions would be the abuse of power for personal gain. *"They have corrupted themselves; they are not His children, because of their blemish: a perverse and crooked generation"* (Deuteronomy 32:5).

A 2018 United Nations report, summarizing comments by Secretary-General António Guterres, said that the problem of corruption "is present in all nations—rich and poor, North and South, developed and developing." The secretary-general stated, "Corruption robs schools, hospitals and

17. Alison Durkee, "Majority of Americans Support Abortion, Poll Finds—but Not Later in the Pregnancy," *Forbes*, June 25, 2021, https://www.forbes.com/sites/alisondurkee/2021/06/25/majority-of-americans-support-abortion-poll-finds---but-not-later-in-the-pregnancy.
18. *Merriam-Webster.com Dictionary*, s.v. "corruption," https://www.merriam-webster.com/dictionary/corruption, and *Merriam-Webster.com Thesaurus*, s.v. "corruption," https://www.merriam-webster.com/thesaurus/corruption.

others of vitally needed funds." The UN report also said that, according to the World Bank, "businesses and individuals pay more than $1 trillion in bribes every year."[19] The World Economic Forum emphasizes, "It is estimated that corruption costs the world economy 5% of GDP a year, equivalent to $3.6 trillion."[20] For example, an expert with the African Union (AU) asserted, "African countries could be losing 100 billion U.S. dollars annually through corruption."[21] According to the United Nations Development Programme (UNDP), "Bribery and 'facilitation' payments are a common practice in most of the Asia-Pacific countries.... In some countries (India, Viet Nam, Pakistan, Thailand) the reported incidence of bribery is dramatically high with rates above 40%."[22] It has also been estimated that Central America loses $13 billion every year due to corruption. That represents 5 percent of the region's gross domestic product.[23]

The moral decline in our world is evident. Corruption has invaded society at all levels. Values are being lost. Standards of behavior continue to deteriorate. In many ways, our global society views what is good as bad, and what is bad as good. (See Isaiah 5:20.) People have lost their sensitivity to right and wrong; behaviors that are morally wrong no longer seem serious and frightening to them because they are constantly exposed to examples and illustrations of them—whether personally or through the media or Internet—put in a positive light.

As I wrote earlier, people are compromising God's principles because they have lost their reverence for their Creator. Many Christian leaders do not exhibit the integrity that the early apostles had. Paul wrote, *"Therefore, having these promises, beloved, let us cleanse ourselves from all filthiness of the*

19. "Global Cost of Corruption at Least 5 Per Cent of World Gross Domestic Product, Secretary-General Tells Security Council, Citing World Economic Forum Data," United Nations, September 10, 2018, https://www.un.org/press/en/2018/sc13493.doc.htm.
20. Lisa Ventura, "Council Mission and Objectives," World Economic Forum, https://www.weforum.org/communities/gfc-on-transparency-and-anti-corruption.
21. "Corruption Could Cost Africa 100 Bln USD Annually: AU," *Xinhuanet*, January 27, 2018, http://www.xinhuanet.com/english/2018-01/27/c_136929533.htm.
22. Diana Torres, "The Future Is Asian, but Corruption Keeps It Mired in the Past," July 17, 2019, United Nations Development Programme: Asia and the Pacific, https://www.asia-pacific.undp.org/content/rbap/en/home/blog/2019/the-future-is-asian-but-corruption.html.
23. Imelda Cengic, "Report: Central America is Losing US $13 Billion to Corruption," Organized Crime and Corruption Reporting Project, October 31, 2019, https:// www.occrp.org/en/daily/11028-report-central-america-is-losing-us-13-billion-to-corruption.

flesh and spirit, perfecting holiness in the fear of God. Open your hearts to us. We have wronged no one, we have corrupted no one, we have cheated no one" (2 Corinthians 7:1–2). Morals and truth alike have been compromised; it is common nowadays for people to claim to have "their own truth" and to try to enforce it in the lives of others, even at the international level. They do not recognize that truth originates in God. Everyone's priority has become their own truth.

Therefore, "*the days of Noah*" (Matthew 24:37) are back, and with them their deviation from morality and total corruption of human character. In Noah's day, God's judgment on the world was the flood, but today, His judgment is beginning with the shaking of all things—the heavens, the earth, institutions, governments, leaders, economies, and more. He is judging those who do not repent of their sin and corruption.

THE END-TIME SHAKING IS GOD'S JUDGMENT AGAINST MAN'S CORRUPTION.

CAUSES OF MORAL CORRUPTION

The underlying cause of the degeneration of human character, which corresponds to a lack of reverence for God, is the egocentrism that mankind inherited with the fall of Adam and Eve in Eden, and which it has further developed in the millennia that have followed. This egocentrism manifests through three characteristics that we read about earlier in the passage from 2 Timothy 3: love of self (in the sense of self-absorption), love of money, and love of pleasure. In their fallen nature, human beings are lovers of themselves rather than lovers of God, and they desire money and pleasure rather than holiness and communion with their Creator and Father.

A LOVE OF SELF

"*In the last days…men will be lovers of themselves*" (2 Timothy 3:1–2). People who are engulfed in a love of self are captivated by the fallen,

Adamic nature—what the Bible calls "the flesh," "the old man," or the "sinful nature." (See, for example, Romans 6:6; Galatians 5:16–17.) The manifestations of the "self" are selfishness, self-preservation, self-absorption, self-exaltation, self-sufficiency, self-righteousness, self-consciousness, self-gratification, self-satisfaction, selfish ambition, being full of oneself, egocentrism, and so forth. Every sin or moral corruption is based on the self, and the self is rooted in the rebellion and pride of fallen mankind. This is the same rebellion and pride that caused Satan to fall:

> *How you are fallen from heaven, O Lucifer, son of the morning! How you are cut down to the ground, you who weakened the nations! For you have said in your heart: "I will ascend into heaven, I will exalt my throne above the stars of God; I will also sit on the mount of the congregation on the farthest sides of the north; I will ascend above the heights of the clouds, I will be like the Most High."* (Isaiah 14:12–14)

Just as our fingers are attached to the palm of our hand, so sin is rooted in the self. Thus, a warped love of self is the genesis of corruption, perversion, and the disintegration of human character. One leads to the other in a spiral of degradation that never ends, always moving toward greater evil and ultimately resulting in eternal damnation unless a person repents and turns to God.

A love of self has led to the disintegration of multitudes of marriages in our world today, as well as to sexual, physical, emotional, verbal, and financial abuse. It has resulted in scores of illegitimate children; rejected, mistreated, and abandoned pregnant teenagers, many of whom resort to abortions; women and men prostituting themselves for money; and people falling into depression, drugs, alcohol, and suicide. Additionally, those who should be speaking out for the moral values that sustain our life on this earth end up giving in to the pressures of the self. For example, Pope Francis, the leader of the Catholic Church, recently announced his support for civil unions of homosexual couples.[24]

Love of self is what destroys society because people think only of themselves and of satisfying the demands of their self-centered and arrogant

---

24. Elisabetta Povoledo, "Vatican Clarifies Pope Francis's Comments on Same-Sex Unions," *New York Times*, November 2, 2020, https://www.nytimes.com/2020/11/02/world/europe/pope-gay-civil-unions.html.

egos, which say, "I am so important that I live by and for myself and no one else. I am first, second, and last; no one else matters. I am the center of everything." In contrast, the Word of God says, *"Let nothing be done through selfish ambition or conceit, but in lowliness of mind let each esteem others better than himself. Let each of you look out not only for his own interests, but also for the interests of others"* (Philippians 2:3–4).

A LOVE OF MONEY

"In the last days…men will be…lovers of money" (2 Timothy 3:1–2). Regarding the love of money, the Bible explicitly says, *"For the love of money is a root of all kinds of evil, for which some have strayed from the faith in their greediness, and pierced themselves through with many sorrows"* (1 Timothy 6:10). It may be clearly observed that the love of money is a strong spirit dominating today's society. Many people work tirelessly to obtain more and more money; other people defraud, steal, cheat, and get involved in shady deals for the purpose of gaining riches. Generally speaking, our contemporary culture thinks that if a practice or endeavor makes money, it is justified, regardless of its morality; as a result, personal and societal values are being sacrificed. For example, each year, the pornography industry is estimated to bring in multiple billions of dollars of revenue in the United States alone, and up to $97 billion globally.[25] However, this industry is based on the moral and sexual perversion of millions of adults, young people, and children around the world. In many instances, its use is not prohibited or prosecuted. It is almost impossible for justice to prevail when the love of money supersedes all moral values, because those who are getting rich through exploiting others will fight to maintain their profits.

A LOVE OF PLEASURE

"In the last days…men will be…lovers of pleasure" (2 Timothy 3:1–2, 4). A love of pleasure will always serve as a root of corruption because it overrides any moral value simply to satisfy the demands of the self.

---

25. Ross Benes, "Porn Could Have a Bigger Economic Influence on the US than Netflix," June 20, 2018, *yahoo!finance*, https://finance.yahoo.com/news/porn-could-bigger-economic-influence-121524565.html; "Things Are Looking Up in America's Porn Industry," NBC News, January 20, 2015, https://www.nbcnews.com/business/business-news/things-are-looking-americas-porn-industry-n289431.

For all that is in the world—the lust of the flesh, the lust of the eyes, and the pride of life—is not of the Father but is of the world. And the world is passing away, and the lust of it; but he who does the will of God abides forever. (1 John 2:16–17)

The love of pleasure reigns over our culture today. For the past few decades, our society's slogan has essentially been, "If it feels good, do it." This seems to be the conclusion of most psychologists regarding homosexuality and other sexual practices contrary to the divine purpose for sex. It is also modern parents' advice to their children when they are unsure about what to do in certain situations. The parents do not guide them in the ways of God's counsel, nor do they talk to them about the consequences of their decisions and their responsibility to themselves and others. Instead, they focus on their children's "happiness" and the satisfaction of their desires. However, once they give this advice, many parents begin to discover that their children's lives are a disaster, but they remain oblivious as to why.

THE SOLUTION TO THE "SELF"

As we know, end-time shaking is not something we can avoid, because it is the result of centuries' worth of judgment for man's rebellion against God and His sovereign plan for the earth. However, we can heed lessons from this judgment, and one of those lessons is this: in order for us to remain in Christ and be the remnant that He takes with Him at His appearing, we cannot remain centered on the self. The moral corruption of the world will continue, but we must turn away from it and pursue holiness instead. By His death and resurrection, Jesus paid for our iniquities and cleansed us from the corruption that was separating us from the Father and leading us to spiritual death for all eternity. Jesus became our propitiation:

Being justified freely by His grace through the redemption that is in Christ Jesus, whom God set forth as a propitiation [mercy seat] by His blood, through faith, to demonstrate His righteousness, because in His forbearance God had passed over the sins that were previously committed, to demonstrate at the present time His righteousness, that

He might be just and the justifier of the one who has faith in Jesus.
(Romans 3:24–26)

In this is love, not that we loved God, but that He loved us and sent His Son to be the propitiation for our sins.   (1 John 4:10)

The solution to dealing with the self is found in what Jesus told His disciples when He announced to them all the sufferings He would go through to save us from eternal damnation: *"Then Jesus said to His disciples, 'If anyone desires to come after Me, let him deny himself, and take up his cross, and follow Me. For whoever desires to save his life will lose it, but whoever loses his life for My sake will find it'"* (Matthew 16:24–25). To keep the self from controlling us, we need to repent of all sin, humble ourselves before God, deny ourselves, and take up our cross and follow Christ. I will now expand on these four points because I consider them vital for calling God's remnant from among the church today.

1. REPENT OF ALL SIN

We have seen that nothing on earth can alter or mend the human heart, which is the essence of our character; therefore, moral corruption is irreversible. Neither religion, the government, philosophy, tradition, or human wisdom can change it. Only Jesus Christ and His finished work on the cross have the power to transform our hearts. The condition of this transformation, however, is true repentance on our part: *"Repent therefore and be converted, that your sins may be blotted out, so that times of refreshing may come from the presence of the Lord"* (Acts 3:19). Jesus's work on the cross cleanses us from our moral corruption, but only if we recognize our sins, repent of them, and trust in His sacrifice on our behalf.

Therefore, the way to overcome the self is to recognize that we are sinful, selfish, and self-centered. Our hearts are corrupt, and we must repent immediately. Jesus began His ministry with this statement: *"The time is fulfilled, and the kingdom of God is at hand. Repent, and believe in the gospel"* (Mark 1:15). If we want the kingdom of God in our lives, we must turn from our evil ways—lies, anger, bitterness, stubbornness, pride, ambition, unforgiveness, drunkenness, sexual immorality, and other wrongdoing—and receive the righteousness of Christ.

REPENTANCE ACTIVATES JESUS'S WORK ON THE CROSS IN OUR LIVES.

2. HUMBLE OURSELVES BEFORE GOD

To humble ourselves before God is to submit to Him and recognize that His ways are higher than our ways, and His thoughts than our thoughts. (See Isaiah 55:8–9.) It is to acknowledge that we depend completely on Him. God alone has the solution for our lives, our families, our country, the perplexities and crises we are facing, the corrupt condition of the human heart, and everything else. That solution is found in the cross of Jesus. This is why God said, *"If My people who are called by My name will humble themselves, and pray and seek My face, and turn from their wicked ways, then I will hear from heaven, and will forgive their sin and heal their land"* (2 Chronicles 7:14). Either we humble ourselves, or God will humble us. We need to make the decision to humble ourselves now.

HUMBLING OURSELVES BEFORE GOD IS THE KEY TO THE HEALING OF OUR LAND.

3. DENY OURSELVES

God sees a person's self-denial before Him as the ultimate sacrifice and proof of their love, total surrender, and obedience to Him. To deny ourselves is to deny what we want, feel, and think in order to give priority to what God wants, feels, and thinks, with the faith that He knows what is best for us. It is to recognize that we have not known how to make the best decisions for ourselves or others, and that we have lost our way, as individuals and as a race. It is to say no to the old way of living and thinking—to corrupt desires, negative habits, bad thoughts, and all that comes from the flesh and the devil.

Again, we live in a generation where many people care only for themselves. Our society is all about instant gratification and "feeling good." To overcome selfishness, we must deny the self, turn our backs on it, refuse to give in to false and corrupt pleasures, and submit to God instead. This goes against the tide of today's society; therefore, when we live in this way, we cannot expect to find approval from our peers and others. Rather, we can expect to be misunderstood and rejected by the world in which we live. It is the price of such denial. Our only approval will come from God. Paul wrote, "*But as we have been approved by God to be entrusted with the gospel, even so we speak, not as pleasing men, but God who tests our hearts*" (1 Thessalonians 2:4).

SELF-DENIAL FREES US FROM MORAL CORRUPTION.

4. TAKE UP OUR CROSS AND FOLLOW JESUS

We may attempt to follow Jesus and be His disciples, but if we do not take up our cross, we will not conquer the self. The cross is the place where we die. It is where we nail all our sins, iniquities, rebellions, pride, arrogance, and everything else that separates us from God. It is where we surrender our will completely to Christ to become His faithful followers. But we must remember that this death does not come without reward, for everyone who dies with Christ will also live with Him:

Now if we died with Christ, we believe that we shall also live with Him. (Romans 6:8)

Most assuredly, I say to you, unless a grain of wheat falls into the ground and dies, it remains alone; but if it dies, it produces much grain. He who loves his life will lose it, and he who hates his life in this world will keep it for eternal life. (John 12:24–25)

AN EARNEST INVITATION

Beloved reader, I invite you today to repent of sin, humble yourself before God, deny yourself, take up the cross of Christ, and follow Him on a path that goes totally against the fallen pursuits of the majority of humanity. Today, most of mankind is on an accelerated path toward perdition. The call to be part of God's remnant is one of repentance and humility. Nobody said it would be easy, but the Holy Spirit is still present on earth—and within us—to give us His strength and power to overcome. (See, for example, 1 John 4:4.)

How will you respond to this call? What will your action be in the face of the corruption that drags down multitudes of people, including many Christians? I invite you to pray with me the following prayer:

> Lord Jesus, today I repent of having lived in the service of my ego, seeking the satisfaction of the self, money, and pleasure. I acknowledge that I have not been on the right path, and I ask for Your forgiveness. Right now, I humble myself in Your presence, longing for the power of Your Spirit to transform me into Your image. I make the decision to deny myself in all that keeps me from You and to take up my cross so that I can follow You. Grant me Your grace to follow in Your footsteps, to endure persecution for You and Your purposes, and to resist every temptation of the enemy. Grant me Your grace to be and to remain a member of Your remnant until You come for me. I know that if I die with You, I will also live with You, together with the heavenly Father, for all eternity. Hallelujah!

END-TIME TESTIMONIES

Nicole suffered a major shaking until she sought God. He brought a revival into her life, taking her from being an abused woman, full of bitterness and anger, to being an example for her daughter and a leader for others looking for change.

> I come from a very dysfunctional family. My parents separated when I was a child. My father never affirmed me or told me he loved me. After he remarried, he cheated on his new wife, remaining

unfaithful and disrespectful to women. My uncles did the same, and my aunts allowed it. All the women in my family lived with men and had children outside of marriage. I grew up very insecure, lacking direction, and without the example of a good marriage or good family relationships. Dysfunction was the norm; it was all I had ever seen.

I fell in love with a man when I was very young. I thought we were the ideal couple, and we had a daughter together. However, the idyll ended when he became obsessive. He wouldn't let me see my family or friends. He would kidnap me so that no one could find me, and he would threaten to kill our daughter if I left him. I spent seven years in that hell! I thought that was normal life; I didn't know any better. However, it all ended when my husband got another woman pregnant.

From there, I moved on to a relationship with a drug trafficker, and he, also, was controlling. Materially, I had everything I wanted—the house, the car, the money—but I felt an emptiness in my heart. One day, while watching television, I heard a preacher talking about God. Suddenly, a great peace came over me, and I knew there was more to life than what I was experiencing. I caught a glimpse of what my future would be if I kept on the way I had been, and I knew I didn't want to continue like that or give that negative legacy to my daughter.

When I went to King Jesus Ministry, God broke my bonds. He took me back to my childhood, to the fears and insecurities, to the places I had walked and how I had let people mistreat me—and He healed me. At King Jesus, I was told that I was valuable and that God had a plan for me. I found joy, peace, and forgiveness, not only from God but also from myself. I was baptized and took the classes for new believers. Everything was going well until it was time for the leadership training. I thought I had nothing to offer, nothing to say or give; but the vision of this church empowered me. I took the courses and started teaching in a House of Peace. There, I began to pray for people and lead them to Christ. Suddenly, this insecure woman, who had been doing everything wrong, was impacting lives with God's love. That gave me the courage to continue.

I went through a long process of transformation and healing so that, one day, I could have a good marriage. God gave me a man who respects and loves me, who doesn't take advantage of me or hurt me. My daughter witnessed my transformation. One day, she said to me, "Mommy, you are more tender. You don't go from 0 to 100 in anger like you used to. I want to be like you." I hadn't realized that she had seen my displays of anger, much less that I had taken my anger out on her. She and the rest of my family saw me leave the nightclubs, the men, and so many other horrible things I used to do. I forgave many family members for everything they had done to me and shared God's love with them. That forgiveness changed me; I had no more bitterness, anger, or reproach against them, but only peace and love. I became an example of integrity, character, and love for my daughter. And a large part of my family today is Christian thanks to this forgiveness and love from God that transformed my life.

Giosue, from Italy, testifies how he and his church have experienced the power of God during the coronavirus pandemic, thanks to the impartation of God's fire they received while attending our ministry's online RMNT Conference 2020: A Call to Revival.

The members of our church have a great expectation about what will happen during this revival, and we know that God is working in the midst of this season. During these difficult times, when everything else stopped during the pandemic—the economy, the country, the world—the church kept going. We have powerful testimonies. When we prayed for people with COVID-19, they were healed. In fact, during the quarantine, a nurse was converted to the Lord. In the midst of the chaos, she went to work faithfully, and she was the only person who did not become sick. All the patients she attended and prayed for fully recovered. She also opened a House of Peace in the hospital; this group is comprised of sixty health professionals. Many doctors and nurses attended because they saw God's protection over their lives and the healings God was doing. We see supernatural miracles take place there. Because of the manifestations, this nurse's coworkers, as well as the doctors, ask her to pray for them for protection and healing. Glory to God!

CHAPTER 4

GOD'S PURPOSES FOR THE SHAKING

As I have been emphasizing, the end-time shaking is inevitable; we are in the midst of it even now. Nature is being shaken like never before, the world economy frequently faces challenges and crises, and moral values are being violently overturned in all areas. The institutions of government, education, science, religion, the family, and more, which were once so firm and secure, are also being shaken, and people are becoming increasingly distrustful of them. Once this global shaking passes, everything will have been displaced; nothing will be where it used to be.

According to an article in the international news section of *Voz Populi*, in just the first eight months of 2020, "in addition to the worrying rates of global warming, there [were] at least eight major catastrophes" around the world. These calamities included the following: globally, the highly contagious coronavirus and all its consequences, which are affecting billions of people; in Australia, the 2019–2020 fires, with an estimated 15,000 outbreaks emitting 400 megatons of CO_2 into the atmosphere; in northern Ukraine, the Chernobyl fires, which took place extremely close to a plant known to have high levels of radioactivity; in East Africa, the locust plague that endangered the food supply of more than 12 million people; in the United States, the alert concerning the giant Asian hornet, whose sting can cause human death; in northern Russia, in the arctic circle, the spillage of 20,000 tons of diesel into a river, whose cleanup could take up to ten years and cost more than $1.5 billion; a dust cloud from the Sahara, mainly affecting Cuba, Puerto Rico, Martinique, and Guadeloupe, which caused "the air in that territory [to be] darkened and [become] polluted, reaching historic proportions"; and finally, in Beirut, Lebanon, the fireworks depot explosions that left more than 150 people dead, 5,000 injured, and more than 200,000 without homes, with material losses of about $3 billion.[26] There is no doubt about it: the world is in turmoil.

Part of the reason this is happening is that certain powerful demonic spirits are now being allowed to run rampant on the earth after having been held back by God until the end times. Since they had never set foot on earth before, we are now seeing atrocities, or degrees of atrocity, that we have never previously seen. God is allowing this to occur in order to shake from our lives whatever does not belong there, including people, things, and places. Only what is true, firm, and grounded in Him will remain. Everything else will be displaced.

While shakings in our lives can be painful and bring us uncertainty, they are also prophetic—helping us to distinguish the true from the false, the permanent from the temporary, and the important from the trivial. However, as I have previously indicated, if we do not understand the purpose of the shaking, we will feel lost, punished by God, and even abandoned. Therefore, in this chapter, we will further explore God's reasons for bringing this shaking to our generation. We must always keep in mind that His purpose for shaking the world is for judgment, with the opportunity for repentance, but His purpose for shaking the church is for purification. Let's now look at some specific reasons for the shaking.

TO REVEAL OUR MOTIVES

God's main purpose for shaking His people is to reveal what is in their hearts, because the heart is where the true desires and intentions lie. This shaking is bringing to light our hidden motivations, and thus it will illuminate why we do what we do, exposing our personal agendas.

26. Samuel Suárez, "Las ocho catástrofes mundiales más impactantes en lo que va de 2020," *Voz Populi*, August 17, 2020, https://www.vozpopuli.com/internacional/catastrofes-mundiales-impactantes-2020_0_1381961973.html. English translation by King Jesus International Ministry.

When God shakes a person, family, church, government, or society, certain elements, activities, and people will be removed. In many cases, the reason they are removed is that they were not approved by God in the first place. We need to understand this so that we will not feel devastated when we lose people from our lives to whom we were close, or when we are disappointed or even betrayed by people for whom we had affection and trust. (See 1 Corinthians 3:11–15.) We must recognize that God is giving our lives a course correction so we can fulfill His purposes for us.

WHEN GOD SHAKES A RELATIONSHIP, WE DISCOVER WHAT IT WAS BUILT ON.

When we experience shaking, it is a time to be honest and transparent before God, because whatever we are trying to hide, He will reveal and expose, often publicly. When something we have hidden is revealed, we have no other option but to deal with it, *"for our God is a consuming fire"* (Hebrews 12:29). Judgment will always come if there is no repentance, *"for there is nothing hidden which will not be revealed, nor has anything been kept secret but that it should come to light"* (Mark 4:22). We read in the book of Daniel, *"He [God] reveals deep and secret things; He knows what is in the darkness, and light dwells with Him"* (Daniel 2:22).

TO PRODUCE POSITIVE CHANGE IN US

God is continually working to effect positive change in our lives, and that is the aim of any shaking, including what we are experiencing personally, locally, nationally, and globally today. Change is constant because everything in this world inevitably changes. Nothing is as guaranteed as change itself; we see this principle in the natural world on earth, in the universe, and in the life of the Spirit. Jesus died on the cross to produce change within us that brings us closer to the Father. Therefore, shaking is part of the very nature of our existence, and we must accept it as such. Again, some people fear shaking because they do not know its purpose; they believe that it will destroy them, not realizing that it is sent to transform them. All shakings sent by God are intended to enable us to progress in developing the character of Christ, including the quality of holiness. Thus, shaking is for our own benefit. We must let go of a mindset that resists shakings and allow ourselves to be molded by God, because *"all things work together for good to those who love God, to those who are the called according to His purpose"* (Romans 8:28).

TO RELEASE BLESSINGS IN OUR LIVES

I challenge you to show me one person in the Bible who was truly blessed by God without having gone through a shaking of some kind. I can guarantee that you won't find any. Take David, for example. Amid a personal shaking, he contemplated, *"When I kept silent, my bones grew old through my groaning all day long. For day and night Your hand was heavy upon me"* (Psalm 32:3–4). Later, David wrote, *"The Lord is near to those who have a broken heart, and saves such as have a contrite spirit. Many are the afflictions of the righteous, but the Lord delivers him out of them all"* (Psalm 34:18–19). When we refuse to yield to the process of being shaken, we also reject the blessing of allowing ourselves to be changed by God. If we recognize what, specifically, God wants to transform in our lives, and if we identify what He wants to remove, we will make room for both the new and the true that He wants to bring us. But again, receiving the blessing of the shaking depends on our obedience and surrender to God in the midst of it.

TO SURVIVE THE SHAKING, WE MUST BE OBEDIENT.

TO EXPOSE WHAT UNSETTLES US

Beloved reader, what situations disturb your peace or move you out of a sense of security? Are you thrown by financial problems? Do you emotionally collapse during life's crises? Are you alarmed by hurricanes or other physical storms? Are you derailed by abandonment, deception, betrayal, or rejection by peers, friends, or your own family? Such shakings reveal what we truly rely on in life. Do you trust in your savings? Do you trust in your material resources? Do you trust in your ability to provide for your family? God uses situations of shaking to help us recognize that we need to place our trust fully in Him at all times. We all need to recognize the areas where we are relying on our own strength or on something in the physical world rather than on Him. God is leading His church to depend on Him as their ultimate Source in *everything*.

In Daniel 3, we read about three young Hebrew men who, having been taken captive to Babylon, were tested during a great crisis. Conscripted to work in the palace of King Nebuchadnezzar, Shadrach, Meshach, and Abednego found themselves in a situation that shook their faith and tested their dependence on the Lord. They were challenged to worship a Babylonian god fashioned out of gold, and they refused. As punishment, the king ordered that they be thrown into a fiery furnace.

The three young men were not moved by the threat of death by fire because their faith was fully in God, and nothing would make them deny His name or worship another god. They said, *"God whom we serve is able to deliver us from the burning fiery furnace, and He will deliver us from your hand, O king. But if not, let it be known to you, O king, that we do not serve your gods, nor will we worship the gold image which you have set up"* (Daniel 3:17–18). What happened? Although Shadrach, Meshach, and Abednego were bound and thrown into the fire, they walked in the midst of the flames unharmed because Jesus, in preincarnate form, was with them. The king said, *"I see four men loose, walking in the midst of the fire; and they are not hurt, and the form of the fourth is like the Son of God"* (verse 25). The king's own men who had thrown Shadrach, Meshach, and Abednego into the furnace had died due to the intensity of the flames; however, the children of the living God were supernaturally protected and walked out of the furnace alive. *"The hair of their head was not singed nor were their garments affected, and the smell of fire was not on them"* (verse 27). Glory to God for the shaking that purifies our faith!

TO REVEAL AND REFINE THE REMNANT

In one of David's prophetic psalms about Jesus, we read, *"I have set the* LORD *always before me; because He is at my right hand I shall not be moved"* (Psalm 16:8). If anyone was shaken during their life on earth, it was Jesus. His greatest and last shaking was when He was taken to hell itself after dying cruelly on the cross for our sins. But He knew that God would not leave Him there, as it says in Psalm 16:10: *"For You will not leave my soul in Sheol, nor will You allow Your Holy One to see corruption."* Knowing that Jesus endured and came through the shaking in His earthly life empowers us to come through shakings, too, as long as we remain His faithful remnant.

Again, what we believe, what we do, and how we act in times of shaking reveal who we are in our inner being. Are we part of the remnant? Are we those who do not cease trusting in God and worshipping Him even under the pressure of crisis, fear, sickness, or another form of shaking? Or are we those who, in the face of the testing that comes with shaking, turn away from God, allowing our faith to crumble? Believe it or not, the world is watching how we act during these unprecedented end times. All eyes are on us. Will you be part of those who fear or those who believe? As in the story of the three young men who defied the king of Babylon, when we choose God above all else, He walks with us in the midst of the fiery trial. The remnant includes those who pass through the fire and are not burned by it; rather, they experience the presence of God at their side, which prevents the shaking from destroying them.

THE FIRE OF THE SHAKING REVEALS THE REMNANT WHO REMAIN FAITHFUL TO THEIR GOD.

TO REVEAL THE END-TIME GLORY

Whenever a shaking takes place, its intrinsic purpose is to reveal God's end-time glory, because God is calling His remnant to be bearers of His glory in the last-days revival. The apostle Paul, who suffered all kinds of persecutions and shakings in his life as a Christian, wrote in his letter to the Corinthian believers, *"For our light affliction, which is but for a moment, is working for us a far more exceeding and eternal weight of glory"* (2 Corinthians 4:17). I believe Paul remembered these words of the prophet Haggai: *"'The glory of this latter temple shall be greater than the former,' says the Lord of hosts. 'And in this place I will give peace,' says the Lord of hosts"* (Haggai 2:9). God is allowing today's shakings for the purpose of showing us His glory, because the former and the latter glory will be manifested together in these end times.

TO REVEAL WHAT IS OF GOD

As I wrote earlier, everything on this earth that was not initiated or established by God will be shaken. For example, marriages that were entered into out of convenience, emotion, or selfish reasons, rather than according to God's will, will be shaken. If this is your experience, seek God together with your spouse to bring restoration to your marriage and start fresh in the Lord. Do everything you can on your part, and entrust the rest to the Lord. Ministers and other leaders, and even ministries and religious organizations, that were put in place by man rather than by God, will also be shaken, for *"not everyone who says to Me, 'Lord, Lord,' shall enter the kingdom of heaven, but he who does the will of My Father in heaven"* (Matthew 7:21). If you or your ministry has been shaken in this way, repent, seek God with prayer and fasting, and find out His will for you so you can serve Him anew under the Spirit's direction. Everything that was established by natural means will be removed; only that which was established by the will of God through supernatural means will remain. God is looking for authenticity. *"The righteous will never be removed, but the wicked will not inhabit the earth"* (Proverbs 10:30).

TO TEST OUR FAITH

Think about a shaking that you went through in your personal life. Once it was over, did you maintain your belief in God? Even more than that, were you strengthened in your faith? (See Romans 3:3–4.) Shakings bring us back to reality from our self-deception, pride, and unbelief, and show us what we *really* believe. Check your faith: do you still trust in the eternal God? Make sure your faith in the Lord has not waned. This is a dangerous time to stop believing in Him! Thank God that the shaking in this world highlights the condition of our faith and gives us the opportunity to repent and believe again. Moreover, as we previously discussed, God is shaking some people who do not believe in Him so that they may still accept the opportunity to repent and be saved. *"Blessed is the man who endures temptation; for when he has been approved, he will receive the crown of life which the Lord has promised to those who love Him"* (James 1:12).

WHAT IS GOD'S PURPOSE FOR YOU?

Everything God does on earth has a purpose related to His plan of salvation for mankind. He does nothing randomly or out of caprice, selfishness, or self-serving convenience. God is always thinking of us, His beloved children. That is why, as we have surveyed in this chapter, it is vital to understand the purpose of the shaking the world is experiencing today. Again, if we are unaware of God's purpose in the midst of it all, we are in danger of falling into the delusion that God has abandoned us or that He is excessively punishing us.

Therefore, amid the turmoil you are going through, seek to understand God's specific purposes for you in it. Perhaps He wants to reveal the condition of your heart or your faith to show you what really motivates you in life. Maybe He wants to expose the truth that you are not currently part of the end-time remnant so you can realign yourself with Him and His ways. Perhaps He wants to reveal to you aspects of His own nature—that He is your Provider, Sustainer, or Healer. Or maybe He wants to bring about a particular change in your life or release a blessing for you as He reveals His glory through you. If we know God's purpose in the midst of the shaking, we will not become bitter or lose our faith; rather, like Daniel's three young friends in the fiery furnace, we will walk with Jesus, and the flames will not touch us. We will come through with our faith stronger than ever, and we will be part of that mighty remnant, that glorious bride, that Jesus is coming for. Let us pray together:

> Dear heavenly Father, I thank You for revealing to me the purposes of the shakings that have come into my life, family, business, society, and world. I ask You to forgive me for my sins and failures,

by which I have offended You. I repent of having clung to things, people, and ways of thinking or doing that do not please You or were not placed in my life by You. Reveal what is in my heart, show me the true place You have in my life, disclose the real state of my faith, and test all these areas so that I can be refined and purified in You.

Today, I make a decision to let go of all that does not come from You and to allow myself to be changed by Your hand. I renounce my old way of thinking and yield my will to Yours so that my mind, my heart, and my entire life may be transformed. I declare Your glory, Your blessing, and Your faith for this end time—in my life, family, work, ministry, and society. In the midst of the chaos and darkness of this world, may I be light to bring others to believe in You and follow You wholeheartedly. In Jesus's name, amen.

END-TIME TESTIMONIES

Carlos Santos of Brazil had experienced several upheavals in his life without understanding their purpose. When he came to King Jesus Ministry, God healed his heart, and he learned to obey the Lord unquestioningly and to see God's purposes for him. Now, he is growing in his knowledge of the Father, serves the kingdom with revelation, and is seeing God's glory in his finances and relationships during this end time.

I came to faith in Jesus about twenty years ago when I was in my thirties. Life situations had driven me to rock bottom, and I prayed to the Lord and asked for a life according to His will. In the span of about five years, I was involved in four different ministries before coming to King Jesus Ministry. Here, I had a very strong encounter with God. I had been very hurt in the past. Many people in previous ministries had failed me, but God healed my heart, and I was able to recommit to Him and serve Him. I stayed in King Jesus Ministry and began to grow and bear fruit for God.

In 2013, I was about to lose my home, having a debt of $500,000 for a house that was worth half that much. The bank wanted to give me a chance to refinance, but the application cost $1000. While praying, I felt the Holy Spirit telling me, "I don't want you to pay that money to the bank. I want you to sow it into CAP." Hesitant to do so, I consulted with my wife, and she said, "God asks you for things that cost you because that is your weak area. Obey so that you can be free." So, I obeyed and sowed the $1000. After CAP, my $500,000 debt was forgiven! God set me free spiritually and financially. Sometimes, the shaking comes so that we will let go of what we are holding on to and can receive the real thing from God.

God's provision didn't end there. I used to work at a law firm, but I was frustrated because I was living paycheck to paycheck. My father had invited me to work with him and then take over his business after he retired, but I had a bad relationship with him. I had been very hurt by him, and I held a lot of resentment and unforgiveness. It is not easy to let go of such emotional pain. However, the Holy Spirit confronted me, saying, "How would you feel if you wanted to give something to your son, and he refused it? You're waiting for your father to die so you can take over his business. Is that coming from you as a Christian?" That helped me take the step of faith and forgive my father. I've been working with him for three years now, and it's been wonderful. I'm making a lot more money than before! Plus, I can be of help, be close to my father, and be a witness.

Sometime later, the Holy Spirit placed in me the idea of earning a six-figure salary. In the world, I had made many investments and lost everything. But the Lord said to me, "Give Me a chance. Invest in My kingdom." I felt I was being assured of a profit because God never lies. So, I obeyed once more and sowed a large sum at CAP 2019. Then, the Holy Spirit led me to sow as if I was already earning six figures. We're talking about $100,000 or more! I agreed and sowed, trusting that God gives to the one who sows. Now I can say that I have finally entered that six-figure level of income, which came about supernaturally. In the midst of the pandemic of

2020, I continue to grow. I have never been so blessed as I am at this time! The economy of God does not depend on natural conditions. Pandemic or not, it is supernatural, beyond human comprehension. Today, I am very happy. I am grateful to the Lord and to King Jesus Ministry, to Apostle Maldonado, his family, and his leadership.

CHAPTER 5

GOD'S JUDGMENT

As described in previous chapters, the global-scale shaking of the nations, the church, the economy, and many other arenas of life testifies to the era in which we are living—the end-time era. All around us, we are seeing last-days manifestations that seem reminiscent of the judgment of plagues God sent to the Egyptians when Pharaoh stubbornly refused to free the Hebrews from slavery in Egypt. Again, researchers, scientists, and analysts can describe various aspects of the turmoil that is occurring in our world, and they can provide some explanations for these events, but they cannot substantially anticipate what is coming to the world, especially in the way of God's judgment.

God's faithful Old Testament prophets always spoke what He commanded them to say. They did not withhold the message, change it, or water it down. Remember that Haggai prophesied, *"For thus says the LORD of hosts: 'Once more (it is a little while) I will shake heaven and earth, the sea and dry land; and I will shake all nations, and they shall come to the Desire of All Nations, and I will fill this temple with glory,' says the LORD of hosts"* (Haggai 2:6–7). And Isaiah foretold, *"You will be punished by the LORD of hosts with thunder and earthquake and great noise, with storm and tempest and the flame of devouring fire"* (Isaiah 29:6). Today, we see the world's news outlets reporting on natural disasters that demonstrate these prophecies are being fulfilled today, often with overwhelming force—in the form of cyclones, hurricanes, tornadoes, tidal waves, raging forest fires, floods, droughts, insect plagues, viral diseases, and so much more.

These are the times that the prophets spoke about and that God's apostles and prophets of the last days continue to announce. The time of God's judgment has come, and it is the duty of the apostles and prophets to carry the church of Christ through these shakings so believers may be purified, built up in their faith, and ready for His coming. Jesus said, *"Nevertheless, when the Son of Man comes, will He really find faith on the earth?"* (Luke 18:8).

At the same time, we must proclaim to the world the need for repentance of sin, and present Christ as the only Savior. Unfortunately, very few apostles and prophets are being the voice of God that people need during this hour. They have the calling for it, but they are not fulfilling their commission. Furthermore, the apostles who have global influence are either very few or, in some cases, are not exercising their influence properly. They are simply being shepherds for their churches and communities instead of also being the voice of God to a world that is in great need. Jesus is coming back soon!

For several years, together with other apostles and prophets who are closely following God's call, I have been speaking about end-time signs, shaking, revival, and the coming of the Lord. God has revealed that I am one of the end-time apostles with the spiritual stature to be His voice in the now. I do not take this calling lightly but instead sense a great responsibility to fulfill it. I feel the call of Isaiah when he said, *"Cry aloud, spare not; lift up your voice like a trumpet; tell My people their transgression, and the house of Jacob their sins"* (Isaiah 58:1).

More believers would be founded on Jesus, the Rock, and not be overwhelmed by the shaking if more apostles and prophets were focused on teaching them the truth about our times. Simply giving people a message of encouragement will not necessarily strengthen their faith, but giving them a message of truth will edify them. Therefore, in times of uncertainty, we cannot resort to preaching about worldly perspectives and facts. Instead, we must proclaim God's eternal truth. The facts can vary at any given time, but the truth in Christ never changes because it is absolute, and it works conviction, salvation, faith, hope, joy, peace, and much more in people's hearts through the Spirit. We need to have a sense of urgency in our time, and return to a fear of God. Again, we are not called to preach about mere information or popular topics. People need to hear the truth of what is happening in the world today—and why. This is the message that will keep the church of Jesus Christ on red alert during these end times.

TRUTH IS A PERSON. JESUS IS THE WAY, THE TRUTH, AND THE LIFE, AND HIS SPIRIT REVEALS THIS WAY, TRUTH, AND LIFE TO US.

SIGNS OF JUDGMENT

I have written this book to help people know that God is using end-time shakings to implement His plans, purposes, and strategies on earth, as well as to separate the members of the remnant for whom Jesus is coming from those who will remain on earth during the great tribulation. Again, we must recognize that God is behind the shaking. Without this shaking, we would not be able to clearly identify His hand of warning and judgment working in the earth in the last days. As we have noted, this shaking was announced by the Scriptures thousands of years ago. It brings glory to God's name because the Lord is orchestrating everything to align with His will. The forms of shaking we are currently experiencing are signs—visible realities that point to the return of Jesus Christ. No heavenly warning sign is invisible or subtle. It must be visible so that it cannot be denied. And, the closer we get to the coming of the Lord, the stronger and more intense these signs will become.

ALL END-TIME SHAKINGS ARE RELATED TO LAST-DAYS SIGNS, JUDGMENT, AND THE GLORY OF GOD.

Earlier, I wrote that the coronavirus—whether it was man-made or animal-borne—is an end-time sign. God knows beforehand what man will do, so He allowed it to happen. Given its global nature, it has prophetic significance, and its effects are closely related to God's judgment of the nations. This virus is an infectious, devastating, deadly epidemic that has impacted over 180 countries. There have been confirmed cases in almost every nation of the world, and, at one point, the entire globe was virtually on lockdown. This is what the Bible calls a plague or a pestilence. In Matthew 24, we see that all these plagues we are experiencing are judgments from God pointing to further events in the last-days timeline: *"And there will be famines, pestilences, and earthquakes in various places. All these are the beginning of sorrows"* (Matthew 24:7–8). They are part of the end-time shaking of judgment that is leading us into the tribulation period. (See verses 9–31.)

When we see a plague beginning during the time of the Passover feast, we can be assured that it is a significant sign from God. The coronavirus exploded across the world just in time for the feast of Passover. If we look back, the shockwave of this current plague occurred between March and April 2020. Passover was from April 8–16. In March 2020, Israel's prime minister Benjamin Netanyahu "described the pandemic as 'a global and national incident the likes of which Israel has never known.'" He also said "the pandemic could turn out to be the worst threat to humanity since the Middle Ages; even the scientists, he asserted, were praying to the Creator for inspiration and salvation."[27]

In antiquity, Passover is the only feast that celebrates an escape. In the end times, Passover is linked to the rapture of the church. *"Watch therefore, and pray always that you may be counted worthy to escape all these things that will come to pass, and to stand before the Son of Man"* (Luke 21:36).

As the plague of the coronavirus continued to reach global proportions in 2020–2021, we saw God's judgment over the world economy. International markets took a hit due to the effects of the pandemic. Many businesses were forced to close, and some industries may never be the same. Even more than this, however, the economic crisis has opened the doors to an apocalyptic event. It has begun to pave the way for the unfolding of the economy of the Beast, or Antichrist, prophesied in the Bible. The antichrist

---

27. "If It Reinfects, Virus Could 'End Humanity,' Netanyahu Reportedly Warned MKs," *Times of Israel*, May 8, 2020, https://www.timesofisrael.com/if-it-reinfects-virus-could-end-humanity-netanyahu-reportedly-warned-mks/.

spirit is setting up a world order and preparing the way for the absolute rule of the Beast. The time will come when goods will be severely rationed: *"And I heard a voice in the midst of the four living creatures saying, 'A quart of wheat for a denarius, and three quarts of barley for a denarius; and do not harm the oil and the wine'"* (Revelation 6:6). People will not be able to buy or sell unless they have the mark of the Beast. (See Revelation 13:16–17.)

If all these signs don't make you believe that we are in the end times and that Christ is coming soon, I don't know what will. Jesus said that when we see such signs, we are about to receive our redemption: *"Now when these things begin to happen, look up and lift up your heads, because your redemption draws near"* (Luke 21:28). As I have pointed out, there are apostles, prophets, pastors, and other Christian leaders in the church worldwide who either do not recognize the reality of Jesus's appearing or choose not to recognize it. Instead, they continue to preach only what the people want to hear, not what God wants to say to them. They do not acknowledge Jesus's return or prepare the church for His coming!

GOD OF LOVE OR JUDGMENT?

God is a God of love, but He is also a God of judgment against wrongdoing. Through His judgment today, He is calling to repentance a world that has rejected Him.

> *But we know that the judgment of God is according to truth against those who practice such things* [various acts of unrighteousness and wickedness]. *And do you think this, O man, you who judge those practicing such things, and doing the same, that you will escape the judgment of God? Or do you despise the riches of His goodness, forbearance, and longsuffering, not knowing that the goodness* ["kindness" NIV] *of God leads you to repentance?* (Romans 2:2–4)

In many places in His Word, God expresses that love and justice are interconnected. (See, for example, Micah 6:8; Romans 3:25–26.) In the passage from Romans 2, we see that, although God is love, this does not mean He wants us to cease repenting of our sins, iniquities, and rebellions. A lack of repentance brings judgment. Paul says that God's kindness, or goodness, leads us to repentance, and this is what enables us to avoid His judgment. Anyone who does not repent cannot avoid God's judgment.

EVERYTHING THAT IS SIN AND DOES NOT CONFORM TO GOD'S RIGHTEOUSNESS WILL BE JUDGED.

Do you believe that God is a God of judgment as well as of love? Some Christian leaders are encouraging people to believe a lie by telling them that there is no judgment. They claim that because God is love, we don't need to repent and change our lives. His love is all that matters, so every-thing will be all right, no matter what we do. Such leaders use their offices to say the opposite of what the Spirit is speaking today, leading people to hell instead of guiding them to salvation and restoration. God will certainly remove these leaders from their positions, and they will have to suffer the judgment of this end time.

It is one thing to encourage people—and there is nothing wrong with this, in itself—but it is another thing to tell them that they need to repent. Most of the time, people do not want to acknowledge their sin before God. Mankind has become desensitized to wrongdoing; people's hearts have become hardened. As a race, human beings are corrupt in mind, heart, and body. And the end-time shaking testifies to humanity's widespread and increasing corruption today.

When people believe that God is only a God of love, they do not believe in His judgment. They know and understand so little about God that if they see or experience His judgment, their argument is always, "How can a God of love allow these atrocities to happen?" They may begin to doubt God's love. They cannot comprehend that He executes His judgment out of His love and character as a righteous King, because they understand love only as complacency and permissiveness. This is mainly the fault of leaders in the church because many preachers have compromised the mes-sage of the cross in order to fill up the seats in their churches. Jesus calls us to repent of our sins, die to ourselves, and change our wrong ways of living. When Christ ascended to heaven after His resurrection, He sent the Holy

Spirit to do the work of conviction and transformation in our lives. He promised this Spirit to His disciples, saying: *"And when He has come, He will convict the world of sin, and of righteousness, and of judgment.... When He, the Spirit of truth, has come, He will guide you into all truth; for He will not speak on His own authority, but whatever He hears He will speak; and He will tell you things to come"* (John 16:8, 13).

Being a judge is one of God's attributes—so much so that Judge is one of His titles. He is the God of judgment, righteousness, and justice, as well as of mercy. *"Righteousness and justice are the foundation of Your throne; mercy and truth go before Your face"* (Psalm 89:14). God always prefers mercy, but mankind's persistent rebellion and disobedience bring forth His judgment. God's judgment comes upon mankind when His grace—the window of time and space for human beings to repent—has been lifted, and man has hardened his heart.

WE MUST SEPARATE OURSELVES FROM SIN SO WE WON'T BE JUDGED BY IT.

Jesus was appointed by the Father to be the Savior and the Judge, for He who saves also judges. He operates in both offices because each represents an aspect of His eternal love for us. *"And He commanded us to preach to the people, and to testify that it is He who was ordained by God to be Judge of the living and the dead. To Him all the prophets witness that, through His name, whoever believes in Him will receive remission of sins"* (Acts 10:42–43). We must fully recognize that God forgives all sins, but He also judges wickedness when there is no repentance.

CAUSES OF JUDGMENT ON THE WORLD

What has humanity done to unleash God's judgment? Why would a compassionate God judge someone He loves? These are questions people ask when they do not understand God's nature as both Savior and Judge. Remember that the reason for God's judgment on the world is the accumulation of iniquity and sin that humanity as a whole has committed in rebellion against Him. As we noted earlier, in heaven, iniquity accumulates, like liquid being poured into a cup, until it is complete and God acts. (See Genesis 15:16; Revelation 16:19.) We discussed how people are committing the following iniquities, causing God's judgment on the nations:

+ Continually harboring evil thoughts and desires

+ Shedding innocent blood and committing other acts of violence

+ Having corrupt character

+ Being morally perverse

Again, as in Noah's time, much of humanity today is desensitized to sin and iniquity. "*Then the* LORD *saw that the wickedness of man was great in the earth, and that every intent of the thoughts of his heart was only evil continually*" (Genesis 6:5). Today, the cup of iniquity is complete, just as it was then. God will soon judge those who have continually been sowing iniquity, lies, deceit, corruption, murder, bloodshed, pride, love of money, love of self, love of pleasure, and more.

The signs of the end times testify to the hardness of mankind's heart. If we understand this, we can see why things are so out of control in the world. Because the human heart has become hardened, God is sending increasingly severe judgments. When mankind persists in sin and does not repent, judgment becomes greater. Earlier in this chapter, I mentioned how the pharaoh of Egypt stubbornly refused to free God's people from slavery. He hardened his heart and rejected God's warnings again and again. "*And Pharaoh's heart grew hard, and he did not heed them, as the* LORD *had said*" (Exodus 7:13). Therefore, God sent harsher and harsher judgments, but the ruler continued to refuse to repent until the judgment reached him personally, taking his son's life. He finally let God's people go, but, by then, it was too late. What sense does it make to wait for judgment to destroy us before we will repent, especially if we're going to have to repent anyway? Let us not wait until it is too late to access salvation in Jesus.

When the sins and iniquities of a person, nation, or world are ripe, God will expose them publicly. This is why all countries are under judgment right now; it is also why so many cases of corruption, sexual abuse, and embezzlement are coming to light. We need to call the church, the nations, and the world to repentance. In a situation where He is bringing judgment, God speaks in a very precise way because judgment is a matter of life and death. This means that God will no longer allow us to get away with our sins. That may seem harsh or extreme to some people, but His intention is to save us from something worse.

REGIONAL, NATIONAL, AND GLOBAL JUDGMENTS

In the Bible, we see judgments occurring on regional, national, and global levels. The judgment of Noah's time was global, just as the judgment is now; that is, it affected all people in the world, not just those in Noah's vicinity. (See, for example, Genesis 7:4.) The judgment on Judah that took them into captivity in Babylon was national. (See, for example, Ezra 5:12.) The judgment on Sodom and Gomorrah, however, was regional; it applied only to the people living in those two cities and their surrounding areas. (See Genesis 19:1–26.)

Throughout the centuries, we have seen various regional and national judgments. In the end times, we will see regional judgments (such as fires, earthquakes, hurricanes, explosions, and so forth), national judgments (such as economic woes and political instability), and global judgments (such as the coronavirus).

So far, we have experienced only partial or preliminary judgments, which give people an additional chance to repent. In these end times, all things are being judged with partial judgments in the form of shakings. People need to turn to God now because there will be final judgments—and they are near. When those final judgments take place, there will be no turning back. Today, you have an opportunity to change your life—to turn from pride, lying, rebellion, witchcraft, sexual immorality, or other forms of sin—and run to Jesus!

A LAST OPTION

In His infinite patience, when God has repeatedly called human beings to repentance but they still have not responded, He uses judgment as a last option. And it is effective because, as we have seen, people often seek God when they face crises. Thus, all such chastisement has a similar purpose: to make people examine themselves, recognize their sinful condition, repent of their sins, acknowledge God, and continually seek the Lord.

That is why we must be very careful not to become a church that caters to the seeker, compromising by comforting people without telling them the truth about their condition before God because we don't want to offend them. When we compromise the truth, when we yield to people's demand for moral indulgence, we become a church without the cross, without the resurrection, and without power—and we risk losing the presence of God in our congregations. We must return to the fire of the Holy Spirit, because it will be our only effective weapon against the spirit of Antichrist that is advancing upon the church. Once more, this is the promise we must turn to: *"If My people who are called by My name will humble themselves, and pray and seek My face, and turn from their wicked ways, then I will hear from heaven, and will forgive their sin and heal their land"* (2 Chronicles 7:14).

Let us fully recognize the condition of fallen humanity: human beings are frail, weak, helpless, limited, and ignorant of spiritual things; they are in desperate need of the Holy Spirit's conviction and guidance to enable them to repent, receive the Lord Jesus, be filled with the Spirit, and exercise God's power on earth. We must cry out to God for His help!

WHERE JUDGMENT BEGINS

However, we must also remember that judgment first comes to the house of God. *"For the time has come for judgment to begin at the house of God; and if it begins with us first, what will be the end of those who do not obey the gospel of God?"* (1 Peter 4:17). There are two types of people in the church: the "wheat" and the "tares," or the spiritually alive remnant and the spiritually asleep Christians. (See Matthew 13:24–30.) When God brings judgment on the world, there is always a remnant within the church that is preserved. The judgment serves to separate the tares from the wheat. This is how God causes the truth to be maintained in the church. The remnant is always kept in righteousness.

This is similar to what happened between Israel and Egypt. When God sent the plagues to Egypt, the Hebrews were preserved, while the Egyptians—especially their government—received God's judgment. Today, end-time shakings are judging the nations, but God is preserving His own in the midst of them so they will be prepared for Jesus's appearing. Through all these shakings, we must recall that, for God's children who love and obey Him, the judgment is a process of purification and discipline, not of destruction.

> *"My son, do not despise the chastening of the* LORD, *nor be discouraged when you are rebuked by Him; for whom the* LORD *loves He chastens, and scourges every son whom He receives." If you endure chastening, God deals with you as with sons; for what son is there whom a father does not chasten? But if you are without chastening, of which all have become partakers, then you are illegitimate and not sons.*
>
> (Hebrews 12:5–8)

Thus, God uses partial judgments to correct and rebuke the remnant in preparation for the coming of the Lord. Otherwise, the bride of Christ would not be ready for the Bridegroom but would be found sleeping instead. (See Matthew 25:1–13.) As we see the judgments coming upon the nations, we need to humble ourselves in the presence of God and judge ourselves to avoid being publicly judged by Him. (See 1 Corinthians 11:31.) Paul wrote, *"When I was a child, I spoke as a child, I understood as a child, I thought as a child; but when I became a man, I put away childish things"* (1 Corinthians 13:11). We must not remain immature, thinking we can be spiritually asleep or keep sinning and have nothing happen in consequence. Every remnant of God's people mentioned in the Bible has always been a sign to the nations, a light in the darkness. We must assume our role as the last-days remnant and be constantly alert to serve as carriers of God's glory.

WHEN GOD JUDGES THE WORLD, IT IS FOR REPENTANCE, BUT WHEN HE JUDGES THE CHURCH, IT IS FOR CORRECTION AND CHARACTER DEVELOPMENT.

CAUSES OF JUDGMENT ON THE CHURCH

We know that God is judging the world for its evil thoughts and desires, for shedding innocent blood and committing other acts of violence, and for its corrupt character and moral perversion. But why does He

judge His own house? We have seen that the reason is not for our destruction but for our correction and transformation. However, people may still
wonder what God's people need to repent of, what they need to correct
and change. The book of Revelation includes letters from the Lord Jesus to
seven first-century churches, disclosing the particular sins and failings of
each church. (See Revelation 2–3.) These sins and failings are just as present in the contemporary church as they were then. Let us review several of
them as we check the condition of our own hearts toward the Lord.

LUKEWARMNESS WITH SPIRITUAL BLINDNESS

*And to the angel of the church of the Laodiceans write, "These things
says the Amen, the Faithful and True Witness, the Beginning of the
creation of God: 'I know your works, that **you are neither cold nor
hot**. I could wish you were cold or hot. So then, because you are lukewarm, and neither cold nor hot, I will vomit you out of My mouth.
Because you say, "I am rich, have become wealthy, and need nothing"—
and do not know that **you are wretched, miserable, poor, blind, and
naked**—I counsel you to buy from Me gold refined in the fire, that
you may be rich; and white garments, that you may be clothed, that
the shame of your nakedness may not be revealed; and anoint your
eyes with eye salve, that you may see. As many as I love, I rebuke and
chasten. Therefore be zealous and repent.'"*   (Revelation 3:14–19)

The great sin of the church today is lukewarmness with spiritual
blindness. The following are characteristics of that portion of the end-time
church that is not yet a part of the remnant: it is artificial, passive, asleep,
casual, spiritless, bloodless, and uncommitted; it compromises the truth;
it accepts sin; it avoids being offensive to, or hurting, people's sensibilities
at all costs; it indulges people's fleshly desires; it lacks God's presence; it is
devoid of God's power; it disregards the fear of the Lord; it is politically
correct; it focuses on entertainment; it denies the work of the Holy Spirit
and the reality of the supernatural; and it waters down the gospel. If people
do not repent of these transgressions, we will see many congregations disappear after this shaking.

I believe in the Word of God. I believe there is a heaven and a hell. I
believe in the finished work of Christ on the cross and the power of His

resurrection. I believe in the manifest presence of God, the supernatural, the blood of Christ, the reality of divine healing and miracles, the believer's authority over the devil and his demons, and the Bible's promises of prosperity in all areas of life. I make no apologies for this! And I openly preach the whole message of the gospel of the kingdom.

"CONVENIENT" CHRISTIANITY THAT HAS DENIED THE POWER OF GOD IS THE REASON THE CHURCH HAS BEEN SHAKEN TO ITS CORE.

FORSAKING OUR FIRST LOVE

As a result of their lukewarmness, people have lost their devotion to Christ. *"Nevertheless I have this against you, that **you have left your first love**"* (Revelation 2:4). When people first receive the Lord, their hearts are flooded with the Father's love, and they fall in love with Him. This is what the Bible calls the *"first love."* Many new believers pray every day, attend all the services and activities offered by their churches, tell everyone about what God has done in their lives, and demonstrate their love for the Lord in other ways. They see God working in every situation of their lives, and they believe everything He says in His Word. However, there comes a time when they face an especially difficult situation, don't seem to receive answers to their prayers, experience the wear and tear of life, become weary from working hard in ministry, or become disappointed with other people, and this leads to a cooling of that first love. A sustained apathy or coldness toward God attracts His judgment. *"Remember therefore from where you have fallen; repent and do the first works, or else I will come to you quickly and remove your lampstand from its place—unless you repent"* (Revelation 2:5). We must cry out to God for a fresh encounter with the Holy Spirit and a new filling of His presence!

LACK OF REPENTANCE FOR LEAVING OUR FIRST LOVE BRINGS JUDGMENT TO THE HOUSE OF GOD.

WILL YOU LISTEN TO GOD'S VOICE?

God's judgment is already coming upon His church, as well as upon the world. We can see its consequences upon individual churches, Christian leaders, and Christians in general. God is revealing who the members of His remnant truly are. Which group are you in: the wheat or the tares? Have you been living in lukewarmness and spiritual blindness? Have you abandoned your first love? Have you embraced false or watered-down doctrines? Do you tolerate the *"profane fire"* (Leviticus 10:1) of contaminated worship rather than worshipping God *"in spirit and truth"* (John 4:23, 24)? Have you stopped watching and praying? (See, for example, Mark 13:33.) There is still time for repentance before the *"weeping and gnashing of teeth"* (Matthew 24:51) of final judgment. The Holy Spirit is calling the remnant back to God. Will you listen to His voice? I invite you to pray a prayer of repentance from the depths of your heart:

> Heavenly Father, I acknowledge that I have lost my first love, and I have been living in spiritual lukewarmness during these end times. I have ceased to watch in prayer. I have stopped doing the works of Christ in the world. I need to repent. I need to return to You with all my heart. Forgive me. Help me in my weakness. I accept and embrace the help of Your Holy Spirit. I acknowledge my need for Your power and grace to renounce all that keeps me from Your presence. Renew in me the joy of my salvation, and make me a new creation in Christ. Draw me closer to Your heart. Wash me of all my wickedness. Cleanse my life from sin, and my heart from all iniquity. Today, I renew my covenant with You to be faithful to You, to follow You, to serve You, and to manifest Your power and presence on this earth to those who do not yet know You. Fill me with Your Spirit until I overflow! Today, together with the Spirit and the church, I cry, "Come, Lord Jesus!"

END-TIME TESTIMONIES

Emilio Rodriguez and his wife came to the Lord when they were financially broke, unable to conceive a child, and on the verge of divorce. They were going through a great crisis, and their life was in ruins. Because they did not have a restored relationship with God through Jesus Christ, the judgment on this world was upon them like a curse. Yet, when they surrendered to Christ, everything began to change for them.

I came to King Jesus Ministry two years ago at Easter when I was going through many struggles. My wife and I were at the point of divorce, talking about how we were never going to be able to have children or run our own business. However, it only took God an instant to turn everything around. When I first encountered Him, He immediately began to work in our lives. I had never met Him before, but the day I arrived at King Jesus, He spoke to me and told me this was the church He wanted me to stay in. My mom had been here for twenty years and had never lost faith that, one day, I would come, too, and meet Jesus.

My wife and I were given mentors who taught us to tithe, give, pray, worship, and fast. We immediately obeyed and applied their teaching. At CAP, God instructed me to sow $1000. I didn't have it! At the time, we lived in a one-bedroom apartment and had limited income. But although we didn't have the money, we promised to sow it. Within two months of our fulfilling that promise, my wife became pregnant. It was a miracle! A few months later, we were invited to be part of the End Time Investors program.[28] God put it in my heart to sow $10,000. Like before, we didn't have the money, but we didn't hesitate to commit to giving it. As soon as we got the money together, we went to church and sowed it. That year, we had our baby, our business, and our house. Now, the blessings are continuous. We have peace in our home; family members come to visit us, and there is always room for everyone.

My wife and I had been married for seventeen years without achieving any of our goals, but with God, we had everything we had dreamed of and more in just two years. Of course, it didn't happen without our being processed through trials and testing. For example, when my wife was pregnant, we were hit by an 18-wheeler truck on the freeway, but we walked away with just a few scrapes.

---

28. This is a program at King Jesus Ministry that raises funds to take the kingdom message to more and more areas of the world.

Then, in the middle of the pregnancy, my wife started bleeding, but we had pastors and mentors who encouraged us, prayed for us, and helped us to pull through. My son was born prematurely, but, by God's grace, he survived. We have seen God do so many miracles! And we can't wait to see what He will continue to do in our lives as a testimony of His goodness.

Luis had turned away from God and fallen into criminal activity. The Lord spoke to him when he was in jail, leading him to repent and be restored. God's judgment took him to jail for the purpose of giving him an opportunity to have his life redeemed.

I am a member of King Jesus Ministry and have been in the ministry for five years. However, one year, I stepped away from God. I stopped talking to my mentors and separated myself from the church. One day, during my backsliding, I was suddenly arrested and charged with a crime. While I was in jail, I heard the Lord speak to me, saying, "You are so rebellious that I had to put you in here so that you would listen to Me." That shocked me because I really didn't want to be a rebellious son. So, I called my mentors and went back to church. In just a few days, God took me out of jail and restored me completely. When I attended CAP, I felt convicted and was transformed.

Today, I am a new man! Now, I just feel His presence and His love. I realized that no matter how far I turned away, He was always there to hold me. No matter what the enemy tells you, hold on to the visions God has given you and the words you have received from Him, because everything will happen just as He promised.

Denis Funes's father was detained by the authorities for not having his immigration papers in order, and it seemed he would be sent back to his home country and not be able to return to the United States. But Denis never stopped believing in God and serving Him. And God did the impossible. His father was not only released, but his deportation order was also canceled.

My dad was detained for eight months in Immigration Services. We went to every lawyer we could find, and they all told us that there was no solution. He was going to be deported. In those eight months, I did not stop serving God. I did not stop leading my House of Peace meetings. My family members and I all kept serving in the church, praying, and believing for a miracle. On my birthday, I was given a prophetic word from God that my dad would be released. I clung to that word and believed in it with all my heart. Two weeks later, against all odds, my dad was home again. God worked a miracle, and we have been able to see His glory shine through this difficult process.

CHAPTER 6

HOW TO AVOID THE JUDGMENT

As we come to the final chapter of part I, let us summarize what we have discussed so far:

+ The Lord is shaking all peoples and nations and the foundation of all created things.

+ Everything that is not established in God is being tested and shown to be lacking.

+ The shakings are related to God's judgment for mankind's accumulated iniquity and lack of repentance.

+ The shakings constitute a sign from God that Jesus's appearing, or the rapture, is near, and that the world is under judgment.

+ God is sending end-time shakings both to judge the world for its moral corruption and to awaken the church from its lukewarmness.

+ Although all the shakings are for the purpose of judgment and justice, they are also intended as a means of mercy for those who will respond in repentance to God's chastisement.

In these end times, the cup of sin has overflowed, and the judgment of God has been unleashed upon the earth. In the Bible, when God was about to send the fire of judgment on the cities of Sodom and Gomorrah, Abraham interceded for them in the hope that God would stop the judgment. However, when fewer than ten righteous people were found in them, the cities were destroyed. (See Genesis 18:16–19:27.)

Today, we know God's final judgment on the earth is already underway; this judgment began with the church but has already spread globally. Both judgments will continue. We've already talked in depth about various regional and global shakings the world has recently experienced or is still undergoing. But consider, for example, the *record-breaking* Atlantic hurricane season of 2020, with thirty named storms, fourteen of which developed into hurricanes, including seven major ones.[29] In another example, think about the fact that poverty is increasing and reaching catastrophic levels for many reasons, particularly the effects of the coronavirus, climatic events, and armed conflict. While much headway to alleviate poverty had been made over the last two decades, "the COVID-19 pandemic [was] estimated to push an additional 88 million to 115 million people into extreme poverty [in 2020], with the total rising to as many as 150 million by 2021.[30]

We are called to do as much as we can in the name of Christ to help the poor, the oppressed, and others in need. (See, for example, Matthew 25:31–46.) However, the only thing that can stop the global judgment is widespread human repentance.

GLOBAL REPENTANCE

Previously, we talked about the need for repentance, but in this chapter, we will explore what this means in greater depth. What is repentance? *Repentance* refers to a change of direction; to repent means to make a 180-degree turn and walk in the opposite direction of where we had been headed. It signifies turning away from sins, iniquities, transgressions, injustice, moral perversion, and everything else that displeases God and has brought the world to its current condition and moment of judgment before Him. Repentance is a genuine and sincere change of mind and heart; therefore,

---

29. "Record-Breaking Atlantic Hurricane Season Draws to an End," National Oceanic and Atmospheric Administration, November 24, 2020, updated June 10, 2021, https://www.noaa.gov/media-release/record-breaking-atlantic-hurricane-season-draws-to-end.
30. World Bank, "COVID-19 to Add as Many as 150 Million Extreme Poor by 2021," press release no. 2021/024/DEC-GPV, October 7, 2020, https://www.worldbank.org/en/news/press-release/2020/10/07/covid-19-to-add-as-many-as-150-million-extreme-poor-by-2021.

the evidence of repentance is *change*. There will be no transformation until there is genuine repentance.

Thus, the solution to all the problems of this world is a global repentance before God on behalf of the church and the nations. Isaiah 30:15 says, *"This is what the Sovereign LORD, the Holy One of Israel, says: 'In repentance and rest is your salvation, in quietness and trust is your strength, but you would have none of it'"* (NIV). Why does something that seems so simple cost so much to do? The truth is, for people to repent wholeheartedly, they require a virtue that is scarcely seen today: humility.

Today, many people's hearts are full of pride and arrogance, which prevents them from repenting. When they are in this condition, their hearts cannot recognize that they are engaged in wrongdoing. In addition, they do not know, nor can they know, what to do in the face of the end-time shakings—they do not realize that only God has the answers for them. Humility alone can lead people to recognize their sinful condition—their wickedness and iniquity—and repent of it. When we do not have enough humility, we need the help of the Holy Spirit, who moves on our hearts, brings us to conviction of sin, and redirects us to God. Or, we need the preliminary help of a great crisis that crushes our pride and leads us to recognize that we are fallible and have sinned against God. Then, we will be open to the Holy Spirit's work of convicting us and bringing us to salvation. When we repent, we give the Lord permission to intervene in our lives. *"Repent therefore and be converted, that your sins may be blotted out, so that times of refreshing may come from the presence of the Lord"* (Acts 3:19).

THE REMEDY FOR PREVENTING, DELAYING, AND STOPPING JUDGMENT IS REPENTANCE.

Once more, there is only one remedy that is acceptable for the situation in which the world finds itself today: repentance before God. Unless we repent, God will not intervene. The plagues—health crises, economic problems, and so forth—that are shaking the world at this moment will not go away or be deferred until individuals, nations, *and* the church recognize their sin and rebellion and respond by repenting. There is no alternative! And as I have emphasized, the *first* arena in which repentance must occur is the church. God's judgment begins at His own house so that His people can then lead the world to repentance.

A CHURCH IN DENIAL OF ITS SIN CANNOT STOP A PLAGUE OR A CURSE, MUCH LESS A JUDGMENT.

A LOST KNOWLEDGE OF REPENTANCE

A major obstacle to preventing judgment through repentance is that many people in the world do not even know what repentance is, let alone their need for it and how to enter into it. Today, speaking about repentance, even in the church, is unpopular. We live in an age where people want a quick fix for their problems, one that does not involve any change, much less sacrifice. This is the perfect trap! Such a mindset never allows them to enter into the freedom of spiritual transformation and a deep relationship with their heavenly Father. That is why, today more than ever, the job of apostles and prophets is to reveal to people their sins, transgressions, and iniquities so that their eyes will be opened to them. Therefore, if you are an apostle or a prophet, *"cry aloud, spare not; lift up your voice like a trumpet; tell* [God's] *people their transgression, and the house of Jacob their sins"* (Isaiah 58:1). When people see their transgressions, they can identify them and thereby have the opportunity to repent and stop the judgment.

Each person, church, and nation will have their own way of expressing their repentance. The important thing is that the change produced by people's repentance be evident as they are convicted and led by the Spirit, and as they grow in Christ according to God's ways. We must all respond to God's call to return to Him by examining ourselves, recognizing our sin, and repenting. We must leave behind lying, stealing, hatred, rebellion, witchcraft, sexual perversion, moral perversion, pride, and all other forms of sin. Only then will God intervene in our lives with His redemption;

there will be a radical change within us, and we will pass from judgment to blessing.

THE COMMON DENOMINATOR OF TRUE REPENTANCE IS CHANGE.

THE WORK OF THE HOLY SPIRIT

While repentance is a fundamental condition for stopping God's judgment, we have seen that, nowadays, people want their problems fixed without having to undergo change or make sacrifices. Yet true repentance cannot be fabricated. Therefore, we *must* have this indispensable element in the process of our repentance: the Holy Spirit's conviction. There can be no true repentance unless it is accompanied by the conviction of the Spirit. Jesus knew this, which is why He told His disciples the following: *"Nevertheless I tell you the truth. It is to your advantage that I go away; for if I do not go away, the Helper will not come to you; but if I depart, I will send Him to you. And when He has come, He will convict the world of sin, and of righteousness, and of judgment"* (John 16:7–8).

Only a person in rebellion, with a hardened heart, with a conscience that is dead to righteousness, will resist the power of the conviction of God's Spirit. We must be careful not to become such a person. If, for example, our hearts have been hardened by disappointments, betrayals, and deceptions that we have suffered—in life in general or within the church—we need the work of the Holy Spirit to heal us and lead us to repentance from resentment and hardening. The Holy Spirit's power of conviction will enlighten our consciences, showing us that we are in a state of sin. The truth is that there is no true repentance where there is a rejection of the Holy Spirit because the presence of God is necessary for transformation.

A GENUINE AND SINCERE CHANGE OF HEART IS THE RESULT OF A TOTAL SURRENDER TO THE CONVICTION OF THE HOLY SPIRIT IN US.

How do we recognize the conviction of the Spirit? And how do we yield to that conviction? The conviction of the Holy Spirit is an internal discernment by which He reveals things in our hearts that do not please God and therefore separate us from Him. While it may take a significant amount of effort for us to recognize our sin, it is almost too easy to reject the Spirit's conviction regarding it if we are not careful. When we feel His conviction, it is very important for us to trust that God knows what He is doing and not turn our backs on what He wants to show us.

The secret to yielding to conviction lies in humility and surrender. If we surrender our wills, we receive the power to repent of what has separated us from God. If we do not surrender, we go on to grieve the Holy Spirit (see Ephesians 4:30) and will only face more judgment and shaking. Please understand that there is a difference between feeling condemned and feeling convicted. Condemnation accuses us and leaves us separated from God, whereas conviction leads us to a knowledge of our true state for the purpose of repentance, restoration with God, and transformation. Sometimes, when we show people their sin, they have no problem identifying it to themselves, but their pride and arrogance cause them to deny it. They proceed to push aside conviction, ignore their sin, and refuse to surrender to be redeemed. This leads to their hearts becoming hardened and being in desperate need of softening and healing.

THE MINISTRY OF GOD'S PRIESTHOOD

The kingdom of God is a kingdom of priests. (See, for example, Revelation 1:6; 5:10.) A priest stands before God in place of the people. In the Old Testament, the priest had the authority to offer physical sacrifices before God on behalf of his own sins and those of the people. When Jesus offered the sacrifice of Himself on the cross, He paid for everyone's sins once and for all. (See Hebrews 7:27; 9:12; 10:10.) The wonderful thing about Jesus's work on the cross is that He has made all those who believe in Him to be God's priests. And now, we as priests offer God spiritual sacrifices, such as worship, giving, prayer, and fasting. *"You also, as living stones, are being built up a spiritual house, a holy priesthood, to offer up spiritual sacrifices acceptable to God through Jesus Christ"* (1 Peter 2:5).

In addition, a priest has the power to bring blessing to people by interceding with God to delay or prevent a judgment against them. However, priests who intercede need to be living justly and righteously themselves because that is where their spiritual authority comes from. Therefore, as priests, we have the right to intercede before God to prevent a judgment only if we are standing in Jesus's righteousness because that position alone is the one from which we can exercise authority and mediate before God.

The church has underestimated the power of the priesthood, just as it has underestimated the power of repentance. All priests and intercessors must stand as bearers of God's presence, calling people to contrition for their sins and, before God, crying out for the conviction of the Holy Spirit to come now more than ever. God's end-time priests—whether they are serving in the home, in the church, in business, in education, in the media, in government, or in any other arena of life—must humble themselves in repentance before God, taking responsibility for the sins of individuals, families, congregations, groups, institutions, peoples, and nations. This is what Daniel, Nehemiah, and others did on behalf of Israel in exile. (See Daniel 9:1–19; Nehemiah 1:1–11.)

However, the sad reality today is that many believers are shifting the blame for the world's problems onto other people or sources. No one wants to take responsibility for their own sins, faults, mistakes, errors, or failures—or the transgressions of their own people group or nation. As a result, God's priests are neglecting their proper functions, and problems and evils remain. We must recognize that, as priests, we are the justice of God in our communities, cities, and nations. Intercession, prayer, and prophecy mold and change the spiritual atmosphere of the earth. Our prayers can change environments and worlds as they shape history. We become intercessory priests of regions and nations when we cry out for justice, repentance, and redemption. We cannot afford to abandon our identity as the holy priesthood God has called us to be. In these end times, we must be more strongly established in this identity than ever. But again, the only way we can function as priests is if we are living in righteousness and holiness before God.

A CALL TO REPENT

As an apostle, with an apostolic voice, I am calling the church to humble itself and repent. I am calling the nations to turn to God, repent, and reject their evil ways. Let us all turn to the Lord! Let us repent before Him now. Let us come on our knees before God with weeping and deep sorrow, with a profound sense of having displeased Him. Let us pray together:

> Heavenly Father, You are full of love and justice. You have been, and continue to be, patient with me and with this generation. I come into Your presence with the conviction of the Holy Spirit that I need to repent of all my wickedness, pride, and rebellion. Right now, I surrender to Your presence. I yield to You my will, thoughts, desires, opinions, practices, habits, and plans. I sincerely humble myself before You. I choose to submit to Your will and the guidance of Your Holy Spirit. Lead me to do and say what You are doing and saying today from Your throne. Lead me to be part of the remnant that is preparing the way for the second coming of Christ. Use me to take the gospel of Your kingdom to all who do not know You and need Your salvation. In Jesus's name, amen!

END-TIME TESTIMONIES

Ricardo Gutierrez, who is originally from Cuba, lived for many years without God, having a life full of sin, crimes, and addictions, and a heart that was hardened. He went from bad to worse and experienced the divine judgment on this world until God came into his life. Ricardo repented, and the judgment was stopped.

> I used to work as a bartender in a restaurant and nightclub. I was a delinquent; I would steal, sell, and consume all kinds of drugs, drink all sorts of liquor, and snort cocaine and crystal meth. Due to this dangerous lifestyle, I went into cardiac arrest one day. I only remember seeing everything go dark. I had dropped dead. It was a struggle, but through the help of medical professionals, I came back to life. God had given me another chance. However, I continued to live a sinful lifestyle. Whenever I consumed drugs, I would drink as much alcohol as I wanted without getting drunk. I would

frequently drive under the influence of drugs and alcohol. This led to my having several accidents, but I would often leave the scene, not caring about anyone or anything else that might be affected.

I was known to be insensitive, with no feelings and no heart, and I hurt my parents many times. They could only cry out to God for my life and the lives of the people around me. The only world that mattered to me was my own. Yet I was always left with a horrible emptiness inside me. There were several times when I wanted to commit suicide because, while I was high, I lived one reality, but when the effects wore off, I was living another reality. Twice, I stood on the bridge from Downtown Miami to Miami Beach, intending to kill myself because I could no longer stand the depression.

However, when I went to King Jesus Ministry, God immediately touched my life, and I decided to turn my life around. The first thing I did was seek out my mother and ask her forgiveness for all the hurt and suffering I had caused her. The next thing I did was quit my job as a bartender. I also cut my hair, and I started to throw away clothes, shoes, and everything else associated with my past lifestyle. I stopped going to all the dark places I had frequented and started walking in the light. My mom couldn't believe the change, but God had truly transformed me. After I had served for a year in the vision of this church, my mother came and was baptized. Two years later, my dad was also baptized.

I had arrived at King Jesus not even having a home—I would sleep inside my car—but the people here helped me. I began to work in the ministry in the maintenance department. One year later, I entered a discipleship program. The Lord took away all my vices. I no longer humiliated anyone. I no longer mistreated anyone's heart. In two years, the Holy Spirit worked in me and completely changed my life. I even met my wife at the church. The people at King Jesus continued to help us with everything. Today, we have been married for ten years. I have a business, a house, a family, and children, whom I guide in the things of God. That is my mission. God transformed my life, and I have seen the manifestation of His glory through my family. All I can do is thank Him for all He has done for me.

Elizabeth Pinchite, originally from El Salvador, has many testimonies of her dependence on God and receiving His help. She has seen judgment removed from her life time and time again, and she now sows gratefully into God's work with the leading of the Holy Spirit.

I have been with King Jesus Ministry since it began. I came in the midst of difficult circumstances, yet my life was changed here. The Lord has allowed me to share the vision of this ministry with others, and I have received several miracles.

At CAP 2018, Apostle Maldonado challenged members of the church to each pledge $10,000 to host a future CAP that would be free of charge for the unconverted. I believed with all my heart and made a covenant with God for that money, as I did not have it. I gave it little by little until I had given the full $10,000. By the end of 2019, my family was opening its fourth business! And everything the Lord gave us, we immediately put at His disposal. I am confident that we help minister to the nations and the world every time we invest in the kingdom.

When I came to King Jesus Ministry, I had been employed in a company for seventeen years, but the Lord began instilling in me the possibility of owning my own company. I believed Him. The first thing I did was to covenant with Him to own my own home, with the promise of using it to host His servants, attend to them, and serve them in everything. Today, I have sown into the lives of a number of pastors, many of them apostles and spiritual sons of the ministry, by hosting them in my home. In return, I have seen their transformation and the impartation they have brought to their nations. They have revolutionized churches and the lives of many people! The Lord later used one of those leaders to help me start my business. God opened doors for me with a man I won to Christ, and it was he who financed my business. He gave it to us, and we have grown it to great lengths.

Our business is dry cleaning. As we handle customers' clothes, we declare salvation over these individuals. If they are going through problems, depression, divorce, unemployment, or health issues, we pray for miracles in their lives. When we started, we didn't have enough advertising, so we prayed, and God brought the customers. As we grew, we also increased our sowing into God's work. We always bought Christian books and videos for our clients, and many people have accepted Christ and been healed and delivered in the stores. For example, there is the testimony of a lady who had breast cancer, and the Lord healed her. Young people suffering from depression have also been restored.

How can you not believe in God in these dark days? During the COVID-19 pandemic, we thought we would have to close our doors due to the quarantine, but when we checked the listing, we saw that dry-cleaning stores were among the businesses that could stay open. We made minor adjustments to our giving, but we never stopped sowing. We have kept all our employees. The Lord did not allow us to fall behind in paying our rent on our four store locations.

One day, we went to a family's home for dinner, and they asked us to pray for their daughter who was feeling sick, and no one knew why. We ministered to her and led her to pray the sinner's prayer. A week later, the girl confessed to me that she had taken three abortion pills that day and could no longer feel the baby. But that night, after we prayed and ministered to her, her baby began to move inside her. Glory to God!

One day, I had a dream in which the Lord showed me a great war in my home involving rebellion and illicit sex. From that time, I began to pray without ceasing for my children. Soon afterward, I learned that my two sons had turned away from the Lord. One of them was in a relationship with a girl that was not of God's will. He lost his job during the quarantine but received a new job three months later. When he took the medical tests to start working, he tested positive for HIV. This news was a shock, but I took courage and immediately made a covenant with the Lord. I told my son that he needed to go to church and be reconciled with the Lord. That week, I could not pray. I just lay on the floor and thanked God. My son had retaken the HIV test, and, this time, he tested negative. Today, both my children are back in God's house and seeking His presence every day.

I know we are in the midst of shaking; it is a reality. My faith, and that of others, is being shaken and tested, but I hold on to the Rock. Everything that is not of God is being removed from our lives. I thank God for our being part of a living church where His presence is in every service and where we are taught to watch and pray with living faith and the revelation of the Holy Spirit!

PART II:

END-TIME REVIVAL IS COMING!

CHAPTER 7

THE HISTORY OF REVIVAL

Over the last two millennia, numerous movements of the Holy Spirit have occurred in various parts of the world. The first and perhaps best-known outpouring happened in Jerusalem fifty days after Jesus's resurrection. The one hundred and twenty disciples who received this first empowerment of the Spirit of God had waited in prayer for the promise of the Father, just as Jesus had asked them to do. (See, for example, Acts 1:4–5.) The outpouring of the Holy Spirit on the new Christian church triggered the first mass evangelization. The apostle Peter preached to the crowds of Jews who had gathered in Jerusalem from around the known world to celebrate the feast of Pentecost, and three thousand people came to Christ. (See Acts 2.) Following this event, *the Lord added to the church daily those who were being saved* (Acts 2:47).

As the centuries passed, the church lost its original purity and experienced ups and downs, including certain times of spiritual darkness when the Holy Spirit ceased to manifest His presence and His works, and the voice of God was no longer heard among His people. Yet, through the millennia of human history, despite periods of dryness and apathy in the church, the Lord did not stop moving to fulfill His purposes. He intervened to show His glory and His salvation to the people of earth. He has always desired to have a close, intimate, and continuing relationship with His children and with all the people He has created. He longs for the bride of Christ to be ready to be presented to the Bridegroom without spot or wrinkle. (See Ephesians 5:25–27.)

Today, we are at the threshold of the final great revival in history before Christ comes back for His church. In fact, as described previously, the moral deterioration of modern society, and unusual physical and spiritual phenomena, have been announcing the arrival of the end times. And many last-days events that were prophesied over two thousand years ago are being fulfilled to the letter today.

HISTORICAL AWAKENINGS

Before we explore the end-time revival in coming chapters, I want to give a brief overview of some of the most outstanding historical movements of the Holy Spirit, as well as more recent awakenings. As we review these outpourings, focusing on prominent revivalists within the movements, we will begin to recognize characteristics of true revival.

THE REFORMATION

In the sixteenth century, a pervasive period of spiritual darkness was broken by a move of the Spirit of God. Men from different cities and countries began to feel the need to preach the true and pure gospel of Jesus Christ, without additions or alterations. This was in open contrast to much of the teaching in the church at that time, which was framed within Catholic paradigms that promoted practices and requirements that went beyond what the Bible teaches for life in Christ.

About that time, Martin Luther (1483–1546), a German monk, was given an academic position to teach the Bible at the new university in Wittenberg. Luther objected to the Catholic Church's commercialization of the faith by selling people "indulgences." Paying for these indulgences would supposedly protect the purchaser—or others on whose behalf the indulgences had been purchased—from punishment in purgatory. A well-known phrase at the time was, "As soon as the coin in the coffer rings, the soul from purgatory springs." Luther called for a debate about this unbiblical practice. On October 31, 1517, he nailed a list of ninety-five theses about indulgences to the door of the Wittenberg church:

This slick church salesmanship of indulgences incensed one young priest, who believed that faithful Christians were being manipulated and the Word of God misinterpreted. A faithful student, he wrote a pamphlet comprised of ninety-five claims that he hoped would inspire scholarly debate on the subject. That pamphlet was titled *Disputation of Dr. Martin Luther Concerning Penitence and Indulgences*, but it went down in history simply as "The 95 Theses."...

Most historians believe that Martin Luther never intended for this argument to go public. It was written in Latin, the language of scholars, and it was pinned to the door of the Wittenberg Castle Church. In that day, the church door served as a "bulletin board" of sorts, and posting to it was a common method for inviting other scholars to engage in theological debate.... As an important agricultural trading hub, whatever happened in Wittenberg was soon spread far and wide. Within weeks, the theses had spread throughout Germany, and within months, all of Europe.

Many identified with Luther's sense of outrage at the corruption and deceit practiced by the church. Once a respected academic like Luther dared to question a practice of the Roman Catholic Church, it was much easier for less-educated Germans to join in the criticism. Luther's writings eventually made their way to the pope, who responded by attacking Luther and eventually excommunicating him from the Catholic Church. Luther's one pamphlet lit the spark that led to the Protestant Reformation. His influence on the church almost cannot be overestimated.[31]

The Protestant Reformation contributed to the radical recovery of teachings both precious and vital to the church, such as a focus on the Bible, through which God speaks His will to His people, and justification through faith in Jesus alone, which is the central doctrine upon which the church of Jesus Christ is founded. In addition, during that time, the Bible began to be translated and preached in the language of the people. Luther

---

31. "A Word from the Editor," in *95: The Ideas That Birthed the Reformation* by Martin Luther (New Kensington, PA: Whitaker House, 2017), 5–6.

himself translated the Bible into German. Previously, the Bible had only been available in Latin. Reformers Martin Luther in Germany, and John Calvin (1509–1564) and Ulrich Zwingli (1484–1531) in Switzerland, among others, trained preachers and sent them to preach in different cities and countries––at the risk of their own lives—so that more people could hear the undiluted gospel message.

The effects of the Reformation can still be felt in many ways today. Currently, we are seeing exponential growth in the Protestant church in certain parts of the world, such as the growth among Pentecostal and charismatic believers in Latin America[32] and the growth of the underground church in China, which we will discuss in a coming section.

THE FIRST GREAT AWAKENING

In the eighteenth century, as part of a multination revival that came to be known as the "First Great Awakening," a movement of God emerged in England. Notable preachers of that awakening were George Whitefield (1714–1770) and John Wesley (1703–1791), both former members of the Holy Club led by John Wesley and his brother Charles during their time as students at Oxford. Whitefield preached in numerous towns in England, Scotland, and Wales, and his preaching was accompanied by signs of the Holy Spirit. He traveled to America seven times, speaking in Boston, New York, and Philadelphia, and multitudes were converted.[33]

This revival was supported by earnest prayer:

> The faith and prayers of the righteous leaders were the foundation of the Great Awakening. Before a meeting, George Whitefield would spend hours—and sometimes all night—bathing an event in prayers. Fervent church members kept the fires of revival going

32. David Masci, "Why Has Pentecostalism Grown So Dramatically in Latin America?" Fact Tank: News in the Numbers, Pew Research Center, Washington, D.C., November 14, 2014, https://www.pewresearch.org/fact-tank/2014/11/14/why-has-pentecostalism-grown-so-dramatically-in-latin-america/.

33. "Eighteenth Century Revivals: The Great Awakening and Evangelical Revival," *Renewal Journal*, April 14, 2014, http://renewaljournal.com/2014/04/14/eighteenth-century-revivals-thegreatawakening-andevangelicalrevivals/; "Overview of Revivals," Revival Library, https://www.revival-library.org/revival_histories/evangelical/general/overview.shtml.

through their genuine petitions for God's intervention in the lives of their communities.[34]

John Wesley described one divine encounter during a prayer session:

After a night of prayer and worship with his [John Wesley's] community on New Year's Eve, something similar to Pentecost hit them in the early morning hours. Wesley recorded,

> Mon. Jan. 1, 1739. Mr. Hall, Kinchin, Ingham, Whitefield, Hutchins, and my brother Charles, were present at our love-feast in Fetter-lane, with about sixty of our brethren. About three in the morning, as we were continuing instant in prayer, the power of God came mightily upon us, insomuch that many cried out for exceeding joy, and many fell to the ground. As soon as we were recovered a little from that awe and amazement at the presence of his Majesty, we broke out with one voice, "We praise thee, O God, we acknowledge thee to be the Lord."[35]

John Wesley was an itinerant preacher for sixty-five years. In his meetings, there were manifestations of the Holy Spirit, and he witnessed healings and deliverances as a result of prayer.[36] Even with all the limitations of his day, John Wesley traveled about 250,000 miles on horseback, preached 40,000 sermons,[37] wrote 250 books and pamphlets,[38] trained hundreds of preachers,[39] and reached tens of thousands with the gospel. His brother Charles wrote nearly 9,000 hymns. John Wesley's life and theology continue to impact the world today: "John and Charles Wesley later became

34. Diane Severance, PhD, "What Was the Great Awakening? Know the Facts & Summary," April 28, 2010, Christianity.com, https://www.christianity.com/church/church-history/timeline/1701-1800/the-great-awakening-11630212.html.
35. Bill Johnson and Jennifer Miskov, PhD, *Defining Moments* (New Kensington, PA: Whitaker House, 2016), 25.
36. Tony Cooke, "John Wesley Saw Some Crazy Miracles!" Destiny Image, https://www.destinyimage.com/blog/tony-cooke-john-wesely-experienced-incredible-holy-spirit-manifestations.
37. "John Wesley," Your Dictionary, https://biography.yourdictionary.com/john-wesley.
38. Cooke, "John Wesley Saw Some Crazy Miracles!"
39. Bill Farley, "John Wesley, 'No Half Christian,'" December 9, 2019, WilliamP.Farley.com, https://williampfarley.com/john-wesley-no-half-christian/.

founders of the Methodist movement, which gave birth to the Holiness Movement and greatly influenced Pentecostalism."[40]

THE SECOND GREAT AWAKENING

In the nineteenth century, during what is widely known as the Second Great Awakening, one of the most prominent preachers was Charles Grandison Finney (1792–1875), who is sometimes called the "father of modern revivalism."

> Finney was a highly spiritual and distinguished evangelist, pastor, and theologian, as well as the most noteworthy nineteenth-century apostle of revival. It is estimated that over 250,000 souls were converted as a result of his preaching.[41]

From his own conversion experience, Finney knew about God's manifest presence and power to save. When he received salvation, he "pour[ed] [his] whole soul out to God," and then, he says, "the Holy Spirit descended upon me in a manner that seemed to go through me, body and soul. I could feel the impression, like a wave of electricity, going through and through me. Indeed it seemed to come in waves and waves of liquid love for I could not express it in any other way."[42]

In the Second Great Awakening, as in the First, prayer was key. Finney wrote these words about the importance of prayer in revival:

> A revival can be expected when Christians have the spirit of prayer for a revival—that is, when they pray as if their hearts were set on it. Sometimes, Christians do not use a definite prayer for a revival, even when they are inspired in prayer. Their minds are on something else—the salvation of the lost—and they are not praying for a revival among themselves. But when they feel the lack of a revival, they will pray for it....
>
> What constitutes the spirit of prayer? Is it fervent words and many prayers? No. Prayer is the state of the heart. The spirit of

---

40. Johnson and Miskov, *Defining Moments*, 20.
41. E. E. Shelhamer, "Preface," in *Experiencing Revival* by Charles Finney (New Kensington, PA: Whitaker House), 8.
42. Charles G. Finney, *Charles G. Finney: An Autobiography*, 1908, 32, 33, The NTSLibrary, http://www.ntslibrary.com/PDF%20Books/Charles%20Finney.pdf.

prayer is a state of continual desire and anxiety for the salvation of sinners. It can even be something that weighs a person down.... A Christian who has this spirit of prayer feels concerned for souls. They are always on his mind. He thinks of them by day and dreams of them by night. This is "praying without ceasing." (See 1 Thessalonians 5:17.) His prayers seem to flow from his heart like water: "O Lord, *revive Your work*" (Habakkuk 3:2). Sometimes this feeling is very deep.

This is by no means fanaticism. It is just what Paul felt when he said, "*My little children, for whom I labor in birth*" (Galatians 4:19). This labor of soul is that deep agony that people feel when they hold on to God for a blessing and will not let Him go until they receive it. I do not mean to say that it is essential to have this great distress in order to have the spirit of prayer. But the deep, continual, earnest desire for the salvation of sinners is what constitutes the spirit of prayer for a revival.[43]

It is said of Finney that his "philosophy of revival, expressed in his autobiography and explained in his 'Revivals of Religion', has subsequently affected thousands of Christians and precipitated revivals around the world."[44]

There were other movements of God during the Second Great Awakening. For example, in the United Kingdom, in the 1830s, a "restoration movement was led by Edward Irving [1792–1834], who strongly believed in the restoration of spiritual gifts and the apostolic ministries to the church." Other revivals occurred in Scandinavia, Central Europe, South Africa, the Pacific Islands, India, Malabar, and Sri Lanka (formerly known as Ceylon).[45]

MINISTRY OF MARIA WOODWORTH-ETTER

According to Pentecostal scholar Meredith Fraser, many women were leaders in the American Holiness movement, which was the cradle of Pentecostalism. These were women who had experienced the baptism in

---

43. Charles Finney, Experiencing Revival (New Kensington, PA: Whitaker House, 1984), 19–20).
44. "Overview of Revivals," Revival Library.
45. "Overview of Revivals," Revival Library.

the Holy Spirit; they established churches and Bible schools, and they published books and magazines. One of the first women Holiness preachers was Maria Beulah Woodworth-Etter (1844–1924) of New Lisbon, Ohio. She is known today as the "Mother of the Pentecostal Movement."[46]

In her book *Signs and Wonders*, Maria wrote, "Soon after I was converted [at age thirteen], I heard the voice of Jesus calling me to go out in the highways and hedges and gather in the lost sheep." However, she said, "I had never heard of women working in public except as missionaries," so she did not know how to go about evangelizing.[47] Maria grew up, married, and had children, five of whom died. After years of hesitancy, she finally surrendered to God's call to preach after being healed of her illnesses. Maria held revival meetings in Ohio and began planting churches. Eventually, she built a tabernacle in Indianapolis, Indiana, in which to hold meetings. In her services, "people danced, laughed, cried, shouted, screamed, and fell into trances that sometimes lasted several days."[48]

Through Maria Woodworth-Etter's ministry, hundreds of thousands of people committed their lives to Christ, and many were healed. After decades of ministry, Maria recalled:

> God…gave me the ministry of healing. He showed me that I was to lay hands on the sick and pray for their recovery. The first person that I laid my hands on publicly and prayed for was instantly healed of an incurable disease and turned out to be a wonderful Christian worker in the meeting. This gave me hope and courage. In my ministry I have prayed for hundreds and thousands of people. Almost innumerable people from all walks of life have been healed of all manner of diseases that mankind is susceptible to. Healing for the body, like salvation for the soul, is in the Atonement and belongs to the Gospel. They should never be separated. I have traveled the continent many times and preached to thousands of people in all the large cities of this country. While always weak in the natural,

46. Meredith Fraser, "Maria Beulah Woodworth Etter, the Trance Evangelist," *Priscilla Papers*, July 30, 2019, https://www.cbeinternational.org/resource/article/priscilla-papers-academic-journal/maria-beulah-woodworth-etter-trance-evangelist.
47. Maria Woodworth-Etter, *Signs and Wonders* (New Kensington, PA: Whitaker House, 1997), 9.
48. Fraser, "Maria Beulah Woodworth Etter."

I followed where the Spirit led and trusted Him for the anointing whenever needed. He has never left me. He bears me up under the anointing and makes me as bold as a lion in bearing witness for my Master.[49]

THE WELSH REVIVAL

In their book *Defining Moments*, Bill Johnson and Jennifer Miskov describe the impact of the Welsh Revival and how God used Evan Roberts to help kindle this awakening:

> The Welsh Revival (1904–1905) was a remarkable, unique outpouring of the Holy Spirit marked by rapid mass conversions and significant social change. In only a few months, a spiritual awakening sparked city transformation, major social change, and Holy Spirit fires that spread to, or were a forerunner to, other great moves of God. Meetings where song, testimony, and prayer occurred spontaneously as congregants followed the leading of the Holy Spirit characterized this revival. As large numbers of people yielded to the lordship and direction of the Holy Spirit, a whole country was turned upside down.
>
> One man who had been praying for revival for over ten years had the privilege of helping to ignite this flame. Evan Roberts (1878–1951) spent much of his early life building a personal history with God. In his mid-twenties, he had several encounters with the Lord that positioned him to step into his calling. During the spring of 1904, God awakened him in the early mornings for three months straight. After journeying to attend ministerial school in the fall of 1904, he was "bent" before the Lord during a meeting in Blaenannerch. While this signifies his defining moment, he was not fully "activated" until a month later when he immediately responded to the leading of the Holy Spirit and returned home. Stepping out in faith activated his anointing in a new way.[50]

---

49. Maria Woodworth-Etter, *The Holy Spirit* (New Kensington, PA: Whitaker House, 1998), 13–14.
50. Johnson and Miskov, *Defining Moments*.

These and many other mighty manifestations of the Holy Spirit occurred as the awakening unfolded:

+ [People] cried with remorse.

+ Prayer and praise lasted for hours, continuing until the next morning.

+ People began to prophesy.

+ When conviction and the fear of God came upon [people], drinks remained untouched in the taverns.

+ Wave after wave of the Holy Spirit affected the society.... Betting and gambling obsession virtually disappeared. In this visitation, it seemed that no one was interested in the distractions of sports or entertainment of their time, because people were now passionate about the Lord.... The letters they sent to one another seemed to carry the very presence of the Lord; when they were read by unsaved people, [these people] were saved, and a movement of the Holy Spirit began in them as well.

+ Holiness and obedience were emphasized, [the people] always desiring to exalt and give glory to the name of Jesus.[51]

The revival spread throughout Wales, and, within six months, 100,000 people were saved. This awakening prompted Christians from many other countries to pray and seek God, and there were revivals in Great Britain, the United States, Scandinavia, Germany, Austria, Poland, Slovakia, Hungary, the Balkans, and Russia.[52]

THE AZUSA STREET REVIVAL

As if by telluric movement, the shock wave of the Welsh Revival reached the United States and moved the foundations of American society. At the beginning of the twentieth century, through the Azusa Street Revival (1906–1915) in Los Angeles, California, the Pentecostal movement was born after a succession of local revivals that began the previous year. The

---

51. "El avivamiento en Azuza y Gales" ["Revival in Azusa and Wales"], Unción de lo alto, https://unciondeloalto.jimdofree.com/los-avivamientos-20/el-avivamiento-en-azuza-y-gales/. English translation by King Jesus International Ministry. This website lists many additional manifestations of the Holy Spirit in the Welsh Revival.
52. "Overview of Revivals," Revival Library.

Azusa Street Revival led Christians to turn fully to prayer, and the Holy Spirit descended. Prayer, conviction of sin, and conversions occurred spontaneously and continuously, bringing unusual growth to the church.

Over the next three years, daily services had to be held because of the number of visitors who came to receive the fullness of the Spirit. No one imagined that this would be the beginning of the greatest and most effective movement the world had ever seen. More than a century later, the Pentecostal/charismatic movement is still growing. Probably no country in the world has been excluded from the effects of this remarkable revival. The results have been extraordinary—hundreds of thousands of people have been converted to the Lord and been baptized in the Holy Spirit.[53]

The Azusa Street Revival was led by William J. Seymour, an African American preacher who began his meetings with a small group from his church. This movement was characterized by continuous and novel spiritual experiences in which miracles abounded. It was common to see people receiving the baptism in the Holy Spirit with the evidence of speaking in tongues. Soon, whites began to join this movement, which quickly became multiracial, something that was rare in the United States due to racial discrimination. The secular media and Christian theologians harshly criticized people's behavior at the meetings. Yet, today, the Azusa Street Revival is "considered by historians to be the primary catalyst for the spread of Pentecostalism in the 20th century."[54]

Many times, the revival services lasted ten to twelve hours. Members of the congregation might object during a sermon if they didn't feel a particular preacher's message was Spirit-inspired.[55] Yet noted healing revivalist John G. Lake said this about Seymour:

> There were doctors, lawyers, and professors listening to the marvelous things coming from his lips. It was not what he said in

---

53. Tony Cauchi, "William Seymour and the History of the Azusa Street Outpouring," Revival Library, https://www.revival-library.org/revival_heroes/20th_century/seymour_william.shtml; "Azusa Street Revival," Revival Library, https://www.revival-library.org/revival_histories/pentecostal/american/azusa.shtml.
54. "The Azusa Street Revival: 1906–1908," Apostolic Archives International, Inc., https://www.apostolicarchives.com/articles/article/8801925/173190.htm.
55. "El avivamiento en Azuza y Gales" ["The Revival in Azusa and Wales"], https://unciondeloalto.jimdofree.com/los-avivamientos-20/el-avivamiento-en-azuza-y-gales/.

words, it was what he said from his spirit to my heart that showed me he had more of God in his life than any man I had ever met up to that time. It was God in him that attracted the people.[56]

Author and evangelist Frank Bartleman (1871–1936), who wrote an account of the Azusa Street Revival, stressed the importance of "heart preparation" for revival:

There is always much need of heart preparation, in humility and separation, before God can consistently come. The depth of any revival will be determined exactly by the spirit of repentance that is obtained. In fact, this is the key to every true revival born of God.[57]

George O. Wood, chairman of the World Assemblies of God Fellowship, wrote an article entitled "What Azusa Had and We Need." He listed the following qualities of the men and women who lived the experience of Azusa Street:

+ Great hunger for God

+ Great love for one another

+ Commitment to the Bible as God's Word

+ Dedication to Spirit-empowered evangelism and missions

+ Commitment to restoring the New Testament church

George Wood concluded his article with this statement: "May God work among us in such a way that Azusa Street will only be a shower compared to what He does in giving the latter rain in the years that lie before us, should Jesus delay His return!"[58]

REVIVAL IN INDIA

Some people assume that the revival in India came after the revivals in Wales and Los Angeles, California, but God was already working in

---

56. Cauchi, "William Seymour and the History of the Azusa Street Outpouring."
57. Frank Bartleman, *Azusa Street: An Eyewitness Account to the Birth of the Pentecostal Revival* (New Kensington, PA: Whitaker House, 1982), 10.
58. George O. Wood, "What Azusa Had and We Need," April 8, 2016, Assemblies of God, https://news.ag.org/en/Features/What-Azusa-Had-and-We-Need.

the hearts of the people of India. The Pew Research Center provides this background to the Indian revivals in the nineteenth and early twentieth centuries:

> Revivals in southern India in the 1860s and 1870s featured charismatic gifts, including glossolalia, or speaking in tongues. These revivals set the stage for pentecostal revivals in India at the turn of the century. In January 1905, missionaries and indigenous Christians, under the leadership of Brahmin convert Pandita Ramabai, gathered in western India (present-day Maharashtra) to pray "for a special outpouring of the Holy Spirit on all Christians of every land."[59]

Although there is much to the story of the Indian revival of 1905, here are some highlights of the beginning of this awakening, the various conditions for revival that they fulfilled, and the manifestations that followed.

> [The revival in India] preceded the Azusa Street revival. Pandita Sarasvati Ramabai (1858–1922), that most famous Indian woman, Christian, reformer, Bible translator and social activist, and in particular the revival movement in her mission, had an important role in the emergence of Pentecostalism worldwide. Ramabai is both significant in the origins of Pentecostalism and in the acceptance of its phenomena among some in the wider Christian community....

> ...After hearing of the Welsh revival and a revival conducted by R.A. Torrey in Australia, she dispatched Manoramabai and Minnie Abrams to Australia in 1904 to observe what was needed, and they returned with the conviction that prayer and "pouring out your life" were required for revival. As a result of their visit, in January 1905 Ramabai instituted a special early morning daily prayer meeting, when seventy women would meet and pray, in her own words "for the true conversion of all the Indian Christians including ourselves, and for a special outpouring of the Holy Spirit on all Christians of every land." The number at this daily prayer meeting gradually increased to five hundred. In July 1905, as she wrote two years later,

59. "Overview: Pentecostalism in Asia," Pew Research Center, Washington, D.C., October 5, 2006, https://www.pewforum.org/2006/10/05/overview-pentecostalism-in-asia/.

"the Lord graciously sent a Holy Ghost revival among us, and also in many schools and churches in this country."… The revival lasted for a year and a half and resulted in 1,100 baptisms of girls at the school, confessions of sins and repentances, prolonged prayer meetings, and the witnessing of some seven hundred of these girls in teams into the surrounding areas.…

The first report of the revival in India entitled "Pentecost in India" was carried in the third issue of *The Apostolic Faith* in Los Angeles. This came from *India Alliance*, a paper of the Christian and Missionary Alliance in India:

> News comes from India that the baptism with the Holy Ghost and gift of tongues is being received there by natives who are simply taught of God. The India Alliance says, "Some of the gifts which have been scarcely heard of in the church for many centuries, are now being given by the Holy Ghost to simple, unlearned members of the body of Christ, and communities are being stirred and transformed by the wonderful grace of God. Healing, the gift of tongues, visions, and dreams, discernment of spirits, the power to prophecy [sic] and to pray the prayer of faith, all have a place in the present revival." Hallelujah! God is sending the Pentecost to India.[60]

REVIVAL IN KOREA

Two revivals in Korea also occurred at the beginning of the twentieth century: the Wonsan Revival Movement (1903–1906) and the Pyongyang Great Revival (1907–1910). Methodist missionaries Mary Culler White and Louise Hoard McCully began to meet for prayer, and their dedication attracted other missionaries to join them. These missionaries, along with missionary Dr. Robert A. Hardie, organized a conference in Wonsan, where the Holy Spirit was poured out like fire, bringing a revival that grew gradually.

---

60. Allan Anderson, "Pandita Ramabai, the Mukti Revival and Global Pentecostalism," *Transformation* 23:1, January 2006, 37, 39–40, https://journals.sagepub.com/doi/pdf/10.1177/026537880602300106.

For three years Dr. Hardie was invited to hold revival meetings in various areas. He was asked to speak at Gaesung Church where he wept and confessed his sin saying, "My soul has been restored, repent, confess your sins so that you may be cleansed from all your sins and become true believers before the Lord. Your faith will be renewed!" Dr. Hardie visited ten mission station centres throughout Korea and gave his prayer talks; and during 1904, 10,000 Koreans turned to God during a time of revival! It was in this year that the Japanese Russian War broke out and so Korea (especially Pyongyang) was overrun by Japanese troops passing through. The revival thus begun continued in power and spiritual results until the middle of 1906.[61]

In 1907, the second wave of this revival, the Great Pyongyang Revival, began. "Pyongyang...was known as a city of wine, women and song." It was a dark city where sin reigned; it even had its own training school for geishas.[62] During the war, the government confined American missionaries to Pyongyang. Gathered together to receive God's favor and power, these missionaries sought the Lord, confessed their sins, and repented, and they prayed for repentance and revival for the Koreans also. Over the next few months, groups of missionaries and Koreans prayed for revival. Then, in January 1907, during meetings at a Bible training conference with 1,500 attendees, some of whom traveled a hundred miles to be there, people confessed their sins, and the Holy Spirit began to flow like a river. Missionary William Blair said that, at one point, "it seemed as if the roof was lifted from the building and the Spirit of God came down from heaven in a mighty avalanche of power upon us." The revival even brought conviction among some of the Japanese soldiers. The society of Pyongyang began to change; it became known as the "Jerusalem of the East." In 1910, Blair stated, "In all Korea today there are no less than 250,000 Christians worshipping God in more than 2,000 places."[63]

The Korean church also experienced huge growth in later decades.

61. "Korean Revivals," By Faith Media, https://www.byfaith.co.uk/paul20102.htm. Information in this article from Mathew Backholer, *Global Revival – Worldwide Outpourings: Forty-Three Visitations of the Holy Spirit* (By Faith Media, 2010).
62. "Korean Revivals."
63. "Korean Revivals."

As the Korean church grew explosively in the 1970s, one congregation has attracted the attention of the churches of the world. That church is the Yoido Full Gospel Church (YFGC) founded by David Yonggi Cho. This church has the largest congregation in the world with a membership of 755,000 by the end of 2007. Cho founded the YFGC in 1958.... Many view YFGC as the base of the Pentecostal movement in Korea....

...The most outstanding manifestation of God's power in Cho's tent church was divine healing. Many were healed from various diseases. Cho's sermons penetrated the lives of city slum-dwellers. Divine healing and Spirit-baptism were the driving forces behind the growth of the church. The explosive growth of the YFGC was not only because of divine healing, but also because the members who were changed by God's power went out and preached the word of God to others.[64]

Today, Yoido Full Gospel Church still has a membership of close to 800,000.

REVIVAL IN TULSA, OKLAHOMA, USA

When he was seventeen years old, Oral Roberts (1918–2009) was supernaturally healed of tuberculosis. After serving as a pastor, in 1947, he held his first public healing meeting and established the Oral Roberts Evangelistic Association in Tulsa, Oklahoma.[65] Roberts began his itinerant ministry using huge tents, which gathered crowds of people "to hear his dynamic preaching and experience the laying on of hands and casting out of demons."[66] In 1951, during a sixteen-day revival in Tulsa, a paralyzed man was healed. Roberts conducted healing meetings worldwide, saying that he was merely a "point of contact to help people release their faith" to be healed by God.[67]

64. Young-hoon Lee, *The Holy Spirit Movement in Korea: Its Historical and Theological Development* (Eugene, OR: Wipf & Stock, 2009), 93, 95.
65. "Our History," Oral Roberts Ministries, https://oralroberts.com/our-history/.
66. Debbie Jackson and Hilary Pittman, "Throwback Tulsa: From Tent Ministry, Oral Roberts Built a University," *Tulsa World*, August 20, 2015, https://www.tulsaworld.com/news/local/history/throwback-tulsa-from-tent-ministry-oral-roberts-built-a-university/article_ffcd9306-b102-5310-9898-912b79506204.html.
67. Jackson and Pittman, "Throwback Tulsa."

Preaching of the word is central to Roberts' teaching on healing. To him, healing faith is directly related to the hearing of the word of God. He was a very dynamic preacher. His faith-stirring sermons in the crusades prepared people for healing.... [People] lined up to be prayed for by Roberts by the hundreds as he prayed like a man whose very existence depended on the outcome of his prayers. He declared his own faith in God as he prayed for each person. Anyone seeing the old black and white tapes/videos of the crusades will witness a man of compassion who was moved by the ailments he encountered.[68]

In 1955, Roberts pioneered broadcasting his healing meetings on television. And, in 1961, he announced that God had communicated to him that he should create a university based on the authority of the Lord and the Holy Spirit. He bought acres of land for this purpose, and Oral Roberts University opened in 1965. Roberts also developed other ministries, such as a phone prayer ministry, in which "more than 28 million calls for prayer have been answered."[69] Today, Oral Roberts Ministries continues the evangelist's legacy with a multifaceted ministry.

REVIVAL IN EAST AFRICA

After a great famine in Rwanda, East Africa, Dr. Joe Church, a missionary from Great Britain, and Simeoni Nsibambi, from Uganda, met one day and began talking about spiritual matters. After praying and studying the Bible together, they consecrated themselves to sanctifying their lives before God. This led to a revival in which people were saved and Christians confessed their sins to one another and forgave each other.[70]

The East African Revival (1930s to present) crossed denominational lines and national borders, later moving into Kenya and Tanzania:

68. Thomson Mathew, "Oral Roberts' Theology of Healing: A Journey from Pentecostal 'Divine Healing' to Charismatic 'Signs and Wonders' to Spirit-empowered 'Whole Person Healing,'" *Spiritus: ORU Journal of Theology* 3, no. 2 (2018), 310, https://digitalshowcase.oru.edu/spiritus/vol3/iss2/13.
69. "Our History," Oral Roberts Ministries; Debbie Jackson and Hilary Pittman, "Throwback Tulsa."
70. Michael Harper, "New Dawn in East Africa: The East African Revival," *Christianity Today*, https://www.christianitytoday.com/history/issues/issue-9/new-dawn-in-east-africa-east-african-revival.html.

This evangelical revival was arguably the most famous and influential African spiritual renewal movement of the twentieth century. It began within the Anglican Church of Uganda through a remarkable partnership between Joe Church and several Ugandan evangelists, and quickly spread to the Presbyterian and Methodist churches of Kenya and the Mennonite and Lutheran churches of Tanzania in the 1940s and 1950s.[71]

Those who were involved in the revival focused on Christ and His power to save:

> The overriding theme of the various revival meetings and Keswick conventions was the message of sin, repentance, and forgiveness by the blood of Christ. Joe Church and his fellow evangelists were said to preach only Christ and Him crucified. Even in the overwhelming presence of the Holy Spirit, they firmly believed that "the Holy Spirit glorifies Jesus and points us to the Blood of Jesus for cleansing when we may have grieved Him on the way."... The revival was a purely Christocentric movement that stressed the salvific power and grace of Jesus Christ.[72]

As of 2006, there were 147 million Pentecostal and charismatic Christians in Africa—17 percent of the population.[73] Today, the impact of the East African revival lives on: "Its effects have been more lasting than almost any other revival in history, so that today there is hardly a single Protestant leader in East Africa who has not been touched by it in some way."[74]

REVIVAL IN PENSACOLA, FLORIDA, USA

"A hunger for God, a love for His people, and a heart for missions characterized the new Brownsville Assembly of God" in Pensacola, Florida,

---

71. "Church, John Edward (1899–1989): Prominent Leader of the East African Revival," Boston University School of Theology, https://www.bu.edu/missiology/missionary-biography/c-d/church-john-edward-1899-1989/.
72. "Church, John Edward," Boston University School of Theology.
73. "Overview: Pentecostalism in Africa," Pew Research Center, Washington, D.C., October 5, 2006, https://www.pewforum.org/2006/10/05/overview-pentecostalism-in-africa/.
74. Harper, "New Dawn in East Africa: The East African Revival."

when it began in 1939 with only twenty members.[75] By 1943, the congregation had tripled in size, and, following a prophecy, the members dedicated themselves to building a larger sanctuary with a missionary vision. Membership continued to grow exponentially, necessitating ever larger sanctuaries. The church developed a prayer ministry, a radio outreach, and missions programs; they also offered Christian educational programs with high-school and Bible-college courses.

Over the years, Brownsville became known as a church of integrity, where holiness, prayer, and outreach to the nations were preached. Led by Pastor John Kilpatrick, Brownsville began praying for revival in 1993. On Father's Day 1995, guest evangelist Steve Hill shared with the congregation about his recent encounter with the Holy Spirit in a church in England. When Hill invited the congregation to pray, God "pour[ed] out His Spirit in an amazing visitation."[76] This awakening was called the Pensacola Outpouring or the Brownsville Revival (1995–2000).

Over the next few months, Brownsville Assembly of God held one service after another, with those attending barely taking time to sleep or work a few hours before returning. News of the revival spread locally, nationally, and then worldwide.[77] Over the years, "The meetings drew over 4 million from more than 150 nations."[78]

The church leadership designed four weekly revival services, and, with the help of other local churches, Brownsville hosted the multitude of visitors who, year after year, arrived hungry for God. "Hundreds of thousands have responded to His call to salvation and a commitment to holiness, and a fresh charge has issued throughout the world for holiness and fresh intimacy with God."[79] Many people moved to Pensacola to live in a continual atmosphere of God's presence. In January 1997, the church opened the Brownsville Revival School of Ministry to train new believers.[80]

---

75. "Honoring Our Past," Brownsville Church, https://brownsville.church/about-us/history.
76. "Honoring Our Past," Brownsville Church.
77. "Honoring Our Past," Brownsville Church.
78. Jennifer LeClaire, "Steve Hill Passes Away After Miraculous Life," *Charisma*, March 10, 2014, https://www.charismanews.com/us/43062-steve-hill-passes-away-after-miraculous-life.
79. "Honoring Our Past," Brownsville Church.
80. "Honoring Our Past," Brownsville Church.

In the Pensacola Revival, we see again that we must fulfill conditions for revival. According to Brownsville Church, the "groundwork" that prepared the way for this remarkable awakening included teaching, deeper prayer, weekly communion, and preparing the spiritual atmosphere.[81]

REVIVAL IN TORONTO, CANADA (THE TORONTO BLESSING)

In 1986, John and Carol Arnott felt God's call to plant a church in Toronto. By 1988, they began Sunday services attended by the members of the small groups they had organized for prayer and Bible study. The church grew, and John and Carol were busy ministering to people, but they felt they were spiritually dry and in need of something more. "We… realized that we had run dry through ministering daily, counseling and doing inner healing and deliverance with people. People were growing and maturing, but it took several years for them to become relatively free inside."[82]

The Arnotts committed themselves to prayer, worship, and Bible reading, and they connected with other Christian leaders through whom the power of the Holy Spirit was being manifested. One of those leaders was Randy Clark, whom they invited to speak at their church.[83] The Arnotts and Randy Clark were seeking God, but they received even more than they had anticipated:

> Arnott invited [Clark] to come to preach four meetings at the then Toronto Airport Vineyard. Clark came on January 20, 1994 and the unexpected happened to the 120 persons gathered there. As Arnott reports: "It hadn't occurred to us that God would throw a massive party where people would laugh, roll, cry and become so empowered that emotional hurts from childhood would just lift off."[84]

---

81. "Honoring Our Past," Brownsville Church.
82. John Arnott, "The Toronto Blessing: What Is It?" *Revival Magazine*, December 31, 1999, posted on the website *John and Carol*, http://www.johnandcarol.org/updates/the-toronto-blessing-what-is-it.
83. Arnott, "The Toronto Blessing: What Is It?"
84. Margaret M. Poloma, "Toronto Blessing," Hartford Institute for Religion Research, http://www.hartfordinstitute.org/research/pentecostalism_polomaart8.html.

This revival known as the Toronto Blessing began at Pastor John and Carol Arnott's church next to the Toronto airport, where guest speaker Randy Clark was ministering. Suddenly the Holy Spirit took over the service. This happened again powerfully day after day for more than a dozen years, drawing curious and spiritually-hungry people from around the world.[85]

Toronto Life magazine called it the city's top tourist attraction of 1994. Attendance swelled into the millions in future years.[86]

What "began with a single service"[87] in a city in Canada became a worldwide blessing from the heavenly Father.

Many of those experiencing the signs, wonders, and miracles of the Toronto Blessing found those same signs, wonders and miracles followed them home…when they returned back to their own congregations.[88]

"Home" for these seekers of God meant nations all around the world, enabling the revival to have worldwide impact: "Visitors and itinerant speakers have now carried the fire…to scores of countries on all continents."[89]

REVIVAL IN CHINA

Over the last several decades, the church in China has experienced tremendous revival and growth in numbers. Author Eugene Bach, who has worked with the underground church in China for many years, explains:

There is a general consensus that the revival in China is one of the largest in the world.…

85. Paul Strand, "Toronto Blessing: 'The Greatest Thing That's Happened in the Church in the Last 100 Years,'" CBN News, June 22, 2018, https://www1.cbn.com/cbnnews/world/2018/june/toronto-blessing-the-greatest-thing-thats-happened-in-the-church-in-the-last-100-years.

86. Bill Sherman, "Pastor of Church That Hosted 12-Year Revival to Speak Sunday in Broken Arrow," *Tulsa World*, November 23, 2017, https://tulsaworld.com/news/local/pastor-of-church-that-hosted-12-year-revival-to-speak-sunday-in-broken-arrow/article_d4b7f492-bb2e-56ff-bbae-14b697986805.html.

87. Sherman, "Pastor of Church That Hosted 12-Year Revival."

88. Strand, "Toronto Blessing."

89. Poloma, "Toronto Blessing."

...Based on the research and observations of my own organization, Back to Jerusalem, I estimate the number of believers in China today to be more than 150 million.

Regardless of the specific numbers, the argument can be convincingly established that China is experiencing a massive revival and has been for the last four decades, and that this revival could be an indicator—one of many other indicators—pointing to the second coming of Christ.[90]

One of the most significant results of this revival has been the Chinese Christians' commitment to fulfill the Great Commission.

China's budding missionary movement was born out of a church that is largely unknown to people around the world. There is still great confusion about what God is doing behind the Bamboo Curtain, but it isn't drastically different from other movements of God in history. Not unlike the past missionary movements of the West, China's surge of missionary activity has been born out of revival fires. There are many similarities between the revivals in China and those that have taken place around the world in recent history, one of them being an intense passion for global evangelism that has sparked multiple missionary endeavors.[91]

The Chinese missionaries, born out of revival, have an increasingly focused purpose. One Chinese leader emphasized:

In 2010, we have seen a huge revival take hold in all of China! I was there in the 1980s when China began its famous days of massive revivals, but I tell you that this revival is even stronger. This spiritual revival is happening everywhere, and we have received a clear vision from God.

Before, it was our goal to train missionaries in languages and cross-cultural skills, but many of the missionaries who had been trained couldn't go because they felt too weak and incapable.

---

90. Eugene Bach, *China and End-Time Prophecy: How God Is Using the Red Dragon to Fulfill His Ultimate Purposes* (New Kensington, PA: Whitaker House, 2021), 22, 24.
91. Eugene Bach, *The Underground Church* (New Kensington, PA: Whitaker House, 2015), 38.

Missionaries have been training all over China for years, but most of them have never had a clear vision of where to go in the Muslim, Buddhist, and Communist world.

Now we are having prayer meetings where God is talking to us clearly and telling us where to go. God is specifically calling people to the western borders and to the minority groups....

Now, believers all over China are seeing visions like the ones that the apostle Paul had. These visions are of specific people in specific countries speaking specific languages.[92]

As Eugene Bach says, the vision of the Chinese underground church, which they call "Back to Jerusalem," is simply this: "to complete the Great Commission and see the return of Jesus Christ."[93]

REVIVAL IN MIAMI, FLORIDA, USA

In this section, I want to share with you more about the revival I have experienced, and continue to experience, in my own ministry, as well as how King Jesus Ministry is supporting those impacted by the awakening. In the late twentieth and early twenty-first centuries, the city of Miami was known as "the graveyard of pastors." There seemed to be little spiritual life in the churches. Congregations did not want to grow beyond two hundred members because people were afraid of being overcome by internal division or growing pains. But it was God's plan to stir awakening in the midst of this lethargic spiritual condition.

God has called me to bring His supernatural power to this generation and leave a spiritual legacy on this earth. He is doing this through an ongoing revival of the supernatural in King Jesus Ministry, its campuses, and its daughter churches, as well as those whom we impact through our ministry. My pastoral ministry began in 1996, after nine years as an itinerant evangelist in Central and South America. My wife and I gathered ten people in our living room to passionately seek God's presence, not knowing all that the Lord planned to do. His anointing began to accompany us, and people started giving testimonies of powerful miracles. In three months,

---

92. Bach, *The Underground Church*, 246–247.
93. Bach, *China and End-Time Prophecy*, 5.

our group had grown to forty people, so we moved to another location—which soon became too crowded, so we had to remodel. The Holy Spirit was manifesting Himself with great power, and we were experiencing so much additional growth that the remodeled space, which could accommodate 250 people, soon became too small as well.

By that time, God had shown us that deliverance was a spiritual weapon He had given us to bring hundreds of lives out of the slavery of sin and to break the curse on the city's churches. The Holy Spirit began to operate an unprecedented awakening in our midst. Just one year later, our attendance grew to more than 650 people. At that rate of growth, even four services on Sunday mornings were not enough to accommodate the large numbers of people. So, in December 1999, we bought a building that would seat 1,500 people. As the revival continued, the Lord brought us additional wisdom, revelation, miracles, deliverance, and multiplication. God was using us to build His kingdom, and He was leading us step-by-step, increasing His presence and taking us from one level of glory to another.

Soon, even in our new building, we reached a point of growth where, although we offered four general services, we could not accommodate the more than 5,000 people who were attending weekly. To address this situation, we bought a piece of land near an airport, as had been prophesied to us, to build our own church building, which we could construct to meet our unique ministry needs. As we built this building, the church grew to 8,000 members, so that even six weekly services were not enough! Hundreds of people who came to attend the Sunday services were giving up and going home because it was impossible for them to find parking spots, and there was no room for them in the main hall or in the additional halls where the service was being transmitted through closed-circuit television.

In just two years, we finished the construction of a 100,000-square-foot building, with a sanctuary that can hold 7,000 people, plus offices and rooms for conducting various ministry outreaches. There was also now ample parking space! We completed the construction without borrowing a penny from the bank; the money came through the offerings of our members and the Lord's supernatural multiplication. God provided for us in this way so we could comfortably seat and serve the people who were the fruit of the revival He was bringing to our ministry.

At King Jesus Ministry, we teach people to have a personal, intimate relationship with God, which can be developed only through prayer, worship, reading the Word, and spiritual warfare. We place great emphasis on holiness, leadership development, and Christian purpose. Our outreach to new converts, along with our deliverance ministry, enables new believers to be set free from demonic oppression so they can fully live out their new lives in Christ.

We also have small groups that meet in people's homes for the purpose of worshipping God and sharing His Word. As you may have noted in some of the testimonies at the ends of the chapters, we call these groups "Houses of Peace." There, new believers can experience God's power for the first time; their bodies and emotions can be healed, and their relationships can be restored. They receive discipleship training through which they are taught to live in a way that is pleasing to God, allowing the character of Christ to be formed in them. Members of the end-time remnant are trained to draw out their leadership potential, as well as to discover and walk in accordance with their divine purpose.

Additionally, we have ministries for children, youth, and families. The latter ministry is specifically concerned with the restoration and growth of the family in each of its stages. Our University of the Supernatural Ministry trains future leaders, whose purpose is linked to one of the five-fold ministry offices of the church described in Ephesians 4:11: apostle, prophet, evangelist, pastor, and teacher. Furthermore, we have a ministry dedicated exclusively to serving businesspeople, in which we instruct believers to manage business and financial matters according to Christian principles. Thus, each emerging leader is equipped to impact the world, thanks to the supernatural revival through which they were given spiritual birth or a revitalized relationship with the Lord.

The impact of what God is doing has been felt not only locally, but also nationally and internationally. We have traveled to many nations to minister, and we also reach people globally through television and the Internet. King Jesus Ministry has gone to many areas of the world that have never before experienced God's supernatural power.

The revival in our ministry first began in the midst of the Hispanic community in Miami, Florida, and then spread worldwide: to other areas in North America, as well as to Latin America, Europe, Africa, and Asia. Thus, a global supernatural movement has been born among people of many races, on all continents. The effects of this awakening are almost impossible to measure because the ministry related to this revival reaches millions of people yearly through television, radio, other mass media, social media, and the Internet. The Supernatural Global Network, which is our worldwide outreach to churches and ministries, provides a spiritual covering for more than 400 churches in 60 countries, thereby bringing together more than 705,000 people under the apostolic mantle of this revival.

By God's grace and favor, we have been entering countries where Christians are harshly persecuted, or where it is difficult to freely preach. However, we feel that God's protection is upon us; He is the one who leads us to go to these nations, and He brings us safely home again. In God's purposes, in every place where He sends me, revival is kindled in people's hearts. People are set free from spiritual hindrances, their sicknesses and diseases are healed, and they are enabled to manifest God's power in their families, churches, cities, and nations. This supernatural revival includes people of all ages and walks of life: students, homemakers, laborers, businesspeople, scientists, military personnel, politicians, and even leaders of nations.

LEARNING FROM REVIVAL

I have written this book so believers will be prepared for the times that are ahead of us, so they will begin to seek the Holy Spirit and His fullness, guidance, and wisdom. As we have seen, times are coming when the earthly knowledge people have acquired will be of little use to them. Only the guidance of God's Spirit will be useful for addressing today's personal, community, national, and international crises.

How can we obtain this guidance? Through repentance and submission to the Lord, which will lead to personal and corporate revival in God's presence. We need to repent of our sins and turn to God with all our hearts; we must seek His presence as we prepare the way for Christ's return.

Before Jesus's appearing, there will be unprecedented revival; the whole world will be shaken, we will see signs in the heavens and on earth, and there will be supernatural manifestations that are clear indications of the end times. Are you ready for revival? Are you willing to apply the truths you've learned in this chapter, seek revival, and be activated to fulfill God's will for your life in these momentous last days?

END-TIME TESTIMONIES

Apostle Calbert Mark from Trinidad and Tobago has been connected with King Jesus Ministry for over ten years. After being activated in the supernatural power of God, he has seen revival in his ministry. To date, he has planted churches not only in Trinidad and Tobago, but also in Venezuela and the United States, leading thousands to be revived and transformed by the power of God.

> Early in my ministry, the Lord showed me that I had an apostolic calling. I knew Apostle Guillermo Maldonado through his books and television programs. After listening to many of his sermons and applying the principles and revelations I received, I knew that I needed more. I felt a strong hunger to attend his supernatural school, the University of the Supernatural Ministry, to be trained.

> This all began ten years ago, and what God has done has been extraordinary. I was sent to Venezuela to plant churches, and I trusted in the Lord to do this work, even though the Spanish language was foreign to me. In the end, God used me to plant twenty-five churches in Venezuela, and I learned the language in a supernatural and accelerated way. While doing God's work in Venezuela, I maintained my main church in Trinidad, which is one of the largest in our city.

> After I discovered King Jesus Ministry and was trained there, revival took hold in our ministry, as well, to the point that we have seen immense growth—in numbers and in miracles, signs, and wonders. I have been able to send more than fifty pastors to various conferences, as well as to the University of the Supernatural Ministry, to receive the teaching and coverage of King Jesus Ministry. Three years ago, the Lord spoke to me about starting to plant churches in the United States. This time, I was ready for the call, and the Lord took me to Tampa Bay, Florida. I applied for

my residency, which was approved within eight months. I built a ministry in Tampa in both English and Spanish.

Since I made the decision to obey God's call, I have seen His hand at every step. I am extremely grateful to Apostle Maldonado, his family, and his ministry for continuing to work in the supernatural and open doors for other ministries to flourish and receive the revival of the Holy Spirit. After the work I did in Venezuela and the evidence of miracles, signs, and wonders, I was ordained as an apostle by my church. The call that the Lord had placed in my heart to be an apostle to the nations is finally a reality. All the glory be to God for what He has allowed me to see and do, and all that He has put in my path.

CHAPTER 8

WHAT IS REVIVAL?

In the previous chapter, we briefly reviewed some of the most important revivals in history following Jesus's resurrection. However, as I have been emphasizing throughout this book, I believe these awakenings were only a prelude to what will be the greatest outpouring of the Holy Spirit before Christ returns. This final revival will be an unprecedented movement, beyond what was recorded in the book of Acts of the Apostles when the Spirit empowered Jesus's disciples to go out and preach the gospel of the kingdom. That was the outpouring of the early rain. But, in the last days, we will see a volume of outpouring that includes that of the early rain and the latter rain together (see, for example, Deuteronomy 11:14), because Jesus always reserves the best wine for the end of the feast (see John 2:10).

We are living during the last hours of the feast of Pentecost, which began when the hundred and twenty disciples prayed and waited for the promise of the Father in the upper room, and which will conclude with Jesus's appearing, when He comes for His remnant. Today, we are seeing a new, gradual outpouring of God's Spirit over the face of the earth. This spiritual movement will increase, creating a widespread awakening in the church and bringing forth the manifestation that we all desire: *"For the earnest expectation of the creation eagerly waits for the revealing of the sons of God"* (Romans 8:19).

I assert that this will be the greatest revival in the history of mankind! Knowing that this revival is coming fills us with joy and expectation, but it also brings up questions like the following: What should we expect during this awakening? What will occur in the end-time revival? Is the church prepared to receive this revival, and does it know how to maintain it?

THE OUTPOURING OF THE SPIRIT IN REVIVAL EMPOWERS US TO WITNESS IN THE END TIMES. THE EARLY AND LATTER RAINS COME TO RIPEN THE FRUIT IN ORDER TO RAISE THE HARVEST OF THE LAST DAYS.

IN A DEEP SLEEP

Researchers, academics, and others have offered various analyses of the condition of Christ's church today. However, as we discussed in part I of this book regarding the end-time shaking, it is easy to look around and see that only a small portion of the church is alive, alert, and preparing the way for the coming of Christ. In general, the lack of revival among believers has caused the church to be in such a weak condition that it desperately needs an outpouring of the Spirit to awaken and revive it, to restore to it holiness and a passion for the lost.

This weakness is due, in part, to the fact that the church has become secularized or "Westernized"—taking on beliefs and values that are contrary to the gospel under the pretext of becoming more civilized. The church's leaders have wanted to satisfy people's demands for comfort and convenience more than they have wanted to pursue the priorities and commands of the Spirit of God. In many ways, the church has ceased to be a spiritual entity and instead has become a "modern organization" in order to fit into today's world. It has passed into the hands of good administrators instead of being led by apostles and prophets who hear what God is saying to His people today and are willing to pay the price of doing His will and maintaining the purity of the anointing and the Word that is preached.

It grieves me that the structure of the church has been shaped to question the reality of the supernatural, rather than to promote it as a demonstration of God's power and grace. Many Christian denominations reject the manifestation of the divine supernatural in healings and miracles, and the idea of the active ministry of the Holy Spirit in believers' lives. They have surrendered to human programs that intellectually oversee what should actually be guided by the Holy Spirit. Similarly, many Bible schools deny the reality of the power of God, teaching that healing and miracles ended with the apostles, because these aspects of God's power do not coincide with modern scientific thinking, which has been raised to the level of being irrefutable for modern humanity. While God does use doctors and medicine to help us, His power to heal has been replaced by modern medicine alone, and His power to deliver by psychology and mental therapy alone. Worship that uplifts the spirit and manifests the atmosphere of heaven has been exchanged for music that stirs the emotions alone. The leading of the Holy Spirit has been replaced by the charisma of leaders.

Some churches are absorbed in inconsequential theological discussions while avoiding what is truly important, such as addressing the absence of God's presence and power in our midst. Therefore, when they encounter someone who does manifest the power of God, they see that person as being false and suspicious, someone who does not come from God. Being accustomed to living according to what is false, they do not know how to recognize what is true.

Because most churches do not see the need for the Holy Spirit, they look for other options to meet people's problems and concerns. As a result, many preachers are full of theories, but they are empty of the Spirit. They teach about God without really knowing Him or having had an intimate experience with His presence. They defend a doctrine of excuses that uselessly seeks to explain why miracles cannot happen today, even though the truth is that these preachers are not prepared to manifest miracles. For this reason, people are barely having their needs mitigated. Preachers are not teaching their congregations about the divine provision available to them, and they are not ministering to their congregations according to that provision.

Thus, today, the power of Christ's resurrection is not being preached or imparted. The person of the Holy Spirit is being grieved and quenched, having been given no place in most congregations. Resisting the Spirit has always been a danger in the church. More than two thousand years ago, Paul warned, *"Do not quench the Spirit"* (1 Thessalonians 5:19).

Additionally, many Christians think that the realm of the supernatural is superstitious, mystical, magical, and abstract because Hollywood's portrayal of the supernatural has given it a fantasy or science-fiction connotation. As a result, globally, people's hunger for the true presence of God and His divine supernatural power has practically disappeared. There is widespread spiritual stagnation! The church lives in a state of numbness, passivity, and lack of commitment. It is alarming that the church is in this condition just before Christ's appearing!

In short, we can say that the lamps are out, and no one has oil with which to light them. (See Matthew 25:1–13.) The apostle Paul exhorted the church in Ephesus, *"Awake, you who sleep, arise from the dead, and Christ will give you light"* (Ephesians 5:14). Many "dead" believers need to be fully awakened. The church needs revival!

And what about people outside the church? The Barna Group, one of the world's most credible pollsters, has been closely monitoring the condition of Christianity in the United States for many years and has given this summary:

> The influence of Christianity in the United States is waning. Rates of church attendance, religious affiliation, belief in God, prayer and Bible-reading have all been dropping for decades. By consequence, the role of religion in public life has been slowly diminishing, and the church no longer functions with the cultural authority it held in times past. These are unique days for the church in America as it learns what it means to flourish in a new "Post-Christian" era.[94]

For many people, Christianity has become merely a tradition. While the church has fallen into a deep sleep, the Lord Jesus has been reduced to

---

94. "The Most Post-Christian Cities in America: 2017," Barna Group, July 11, 2017, https://www.barna.com/research/post-christian-cities-america-2017/.

a historical figure; a legend; just another prophet or teacher; a God of the past, and not of the present.

We desperately need revival to bring the church back to life so we can be witnesses in our communities and nations. We must give room to the Spirit of God and let Him act freely in our congregations. Again, while many believers need revival, the questions are: Do they know they need awakening? And do they know what a Holy Spirit revival is?

WHILE THE CHURCH HAS FALLEN INTO A DEEP SLEEP, THE LORD JESUS HAS BEEN REDUCED TO A HISTORICAL FIGURE; A LEGEND; JUST ANOTHER PROPHET OR TEACHER; A GOD OF THE PAST, AND NOT OF THE PRESENT.

DEFINING REVIVAL

The dictionary defines the word *revive* as "to bring back to life or consciousness; resuscitate" and "to give new health, strength, or spirit to."[95] For the church, to experience revival means to be restored to the life of the Spirit, which the church once had but lost. Thousands of years ago, the psalmist implored, *"Will You not revive us again, that Your people may rejoice in You?"* (Psalm 85:6). And the prophet Hosea invited God's people, *"Come, and let us return to the LORD; for He has torn, but He will heal us; He has stricken, but He will bind us up. After two days He will revive us; on the third day He will raise us up, that we may live in His sight"* (Hosea 6:1–2). The Hebrew term translated *"revive"* in these passages is *chayah*, among whose meanings are "to live," "to have life," "to remain alive," "to sustain life," "to live (prosperously)," "to quicken," "to restore (to health)," or "to restore to life."[96]

---

95. *American Heritage® Dictionary of the English Language, Fifth Edition*, s.v. "revive," https://www.thefreedictionary.com/revive.
96. *Strong's Exhaustive Concordance of the Bible*, H2421, Blue Letter Bible, https://www.blueletterbible.org/lexicon/h2421/nkjv/wlc/0-1/.

The Scriptures affirm that the Lord Jesus bequeathed to the church all that He has. (See, for example, Romans 8:32.) In accordance with this enduement, the early church exhibited revival power. The move of the Spirit, with miracles, signs, and wonders, spread the gospel far beyond the borders of Jerusalem. (See, for example, Acts 8:4–7, 12–17; 11:19–21; Acts 27–28; Hebrews 2:3–4.) For Jesus's followers, the manifestation of the supernatural was a way of life, not an isolated event. The church was born—and was able to continue Jesus's ministry on earth—from the outpouring of the Holy Spirit! But, again, the sad fact today is that, for the most part, the supernatural work of the Spirit in the church has been lost.

It is abundantly clear that a new spiritual awakening is needed. Revival comes to breathe life into and restore all that is dead in the church—our faith, our intimate relationship with God, our first love of Jesus, the life of the Spirit, and so on. "*O LORD, I have heard Your speech and was afraid; O LORD, revive Your work in the midst of the years! In the midst of the years make it known; in wrath remember mercy*" (Habakkuk 3:2).

REVIVAL WAS ALL THE CHURCH HAD IN THE BEGINNING, BUT IT HAS LOST IT. IT WILL TAKE A NEW REVIVAL TO BRING THE CHURCH BACK TO LIFE.

OPEN HEAVENLY PORTALS

Every outpouring of the Holy Spirit begins with a heavenly portal being opened over a certain place: a city, region, territory, or nation. That is what happened at Pentecost in the upper room, where, as I mentioned earlier, one hundred and twenty followers of Jesus prayed and waited for the manifestation of the promise He had made to them.

When the Day of Pentecost had fully come, they were all with one accord in one place. And suddenly there came a sound from heaven, as of a rushing mighty wind, and it filled the whole house where they were sitting. Then there appeared to them divided tongues, as of fire, and one sat upon each of them. And they were all filled with the Holy Spirit and began to speak with other tongues, as the Spirit gave them utterance. (Acts 2:1–4)

Through this portal that opened between heaven and earth, the Holy Spirit was poured out upon God's people. The message this outpouring brought was announced to mankind through the preaching of the gospel and the manifestation of God's supernatural power. The Spirit of God reminded the disciples of all that Jesus had taught them (see John 14:26), and that is what they went out to preach to the world. The result was a spiritual awakening and empowerment that prompted the disciples to boldly testify to what the Holy Spirit was saying and doing in that day.

EVERY REVIVAL PRODUCES A SPIRITUAL AWAKENING IN THE CHURCH AND IN THE WORLD, WITH THE EVIDENCE OF VISIBLE SUPERNATURAL ACTIVITY MANIFESTED IN THE NOW.

Revival is available for every person; however, it is important to remember that not everything in our lives or in the lives of our communities and nations will be revived. For example, what God has judged will not be revived, nor will what is linked to the desires of the flesh. In revival, many things will disappear from the ecclesiastical environment because they are not in accordance with the Spirit. Some people will not even be revived unless they repent.

And it shall be that if you earnestly obey My commandments which I command you today, to love the LORD your God and serve Him with all your heart and with all your soul, then I will give you the rain for your land in its season, the early rain and the latter rain, that you may gather in your grain, your new wine, and your oil.
(Deuteronomy 11:13–14)

And it shall come to pass that whoever calls on the name of the LORD shall be saved. For in Mount Zion and in Jerusalem there shall be

> *deliverance, as the* LORD *has said, among the remnant whom the* LORD
> *calls.* (Joel 2:32)

TRUE REVIVAL

Revival is an activity of the Holy Spirit, and therefore it is supernatural. It is what the Spirit is working in the now. If you believe that you are already experiencing revival in your life, in your home, or in your ministry, but you aren't experiencing any supernatural activity, you may be feeling emotion, but it is not true revival.

Revival occurs when the church is revitalized in its relationship with God because it is filled with the Spirit. When this happens, individuals, families, and entire communities are transformed; there are tangible changes, and miracles, healings, and salvations occur. People renew their faith in God; churches prosper in holiness; believers enter into powerful worship; there are *rhema* words[97] and prophetic visions; thousands are baptized in water and in the Holy Spirit; there is discipleship and spiritual growth; there is palpable, demonstrable love between believers; there are financial miracles; there is growth and multiplication in all areas. This is true revival. Where there was once conformity to worldly thinking, deep spiritual slumber, and sterility, now there is life and good fruit in abundance. Jesus said, *"The Spirit of the* LORD *is upon Me, because He has anointed Me to preach the gospel to the poor; He has sent Me to heal the brokenhearted, to proclaim liberty to the captives and recovery of sight to the blind, to set at liberty those who are oppressed"* (Luke 4:18).

All revival begins in the heart. If the heart is not transformed, there is no awakening. Even if there is much activity in the church, this does not guarantee revival. For awakening to occur, there must be a radical change from the inside out. People might feel God's presence, perceive the supernatural atmosphere, cry, and be moved, but if their hearts do not surrender to the Lord, if there is no genuine repentance or visible change in their

---

97. A *rhema* word is a word from God for today, for a specific situation. It will always be in agreement with God's written Word. One example of a *rhema* word is when the Holy Spirit causes the written Scriptures to come alive in meaning for us, with application for our present circumstances. Another example is a prophetic word given through the Spirit for an individual believer or the church.

lives, there is simply no revival. I say this because, as I minister around the world, I often see many people touched but few changed. Countless people surrender their emotions but not their hearts. They will experience true restoration when they surrender their hearts completely to the Father to be transformed in His presence. Then they will be able to continuously live in that transformation.

A church in revival is a church totally centered on God's presence, because when the church enters into His presence, it needs nothing else. *"One thing I have desired of the LORD, that will I seek: that I may dwell in the house of the LORD all the days of my life, to behold the beauty of the LORD, and to inquire in His temple"* (Psalm 27:4). We have taught people to respond to biblical knowledge but not to God's presence. When people are aware of His presence, they do not expect someone else to lay hands on them for a touch from God; instead, they go directly to the Father to receive from Him. God's presence is a place of revelation, rest, peace, and change. It is where the supernatural is most natural, and where nothing that we need is lacking. Therefore, we must reeducate people so that they learn to continually seek, pursue, and live in God's presence—not as a onetime experience but as a way of life.

Dear reader, I invite you to do an assessment of your heart today. Make sure that there is no sin or iniquity keeping you from living continually in God's presence. Iniquity causes God to hide His face from us: *"Behold, the LORD's hand is not shortened, that it cannot save; nor His ear heavy, that it cannot hear. But your iniquities have separated you from your God; and your sins have hidden His face from you, so that He will not hear"* (Isaiah 59:1–2). The more sin there is—in our individual lives or in the collective lives of the members of our churches—the less of a presence of God there is, to the extent that we can be cut off from His presence. The Lord removes His presence when we do not repent of our sins. Conversely, the less sin there is, the more of God's presence we can enjoy.

SIN REMOVES US FROM GOD'S PRESENCE, BUT REPENTANCE RETURNS US TO IT.

WHEN WILL THE END-TIME REVIVAL BEGIN?

The end-time revival will begin immediately after the final global shaking:

> *For thus says the LORD of hosts: "Once more (it is a little while) I will shake heaven and earth, the sea and dry land; and I will shake all nations, and they shall come to the Desire of All Nations, and I will fill this temple with glory," says the LORD of hosts. "The silver is Mine, and the gold is Mine," says the LORD of hosts. "The glory of this latter temple shall be greater than the former," says the LORD of hosts. "And in this place I will give peace," says the LORD of hosts.* (Haggai 2:6–9)

As we saw in part I of this book, the above passage teaches us that every dimension and sphere of life on earth will be shaken; everything that has life will be affected. It is not only nature that will be shaken but the economy as well. When God proclaims that the silver and gold belong to Him, He is saying that what man thinks he possesses actually belongs to Him. God will shake everything before His house is filled with end-time glory. Then the last-days revival will begin.

Remember that, during the final shaking, the Lord will manifest the work of the Holy Spirit even more actively than when the Spirit came to establish the church. He will open portals through which He will pour out His Spirit with a potency never before seen, and He will endow evangelists with power. Evangelism will become more effective, because in the midst of the world's disorientation, despair, anxiety, loss of focus, perplexity, and lack of answers for its crises, people will have no choice but to seek God. Something will occur like what happened after the terrorist attacks of September 11, 2001: churches were filled with people looking for security, peace, and protection in God. However, this time, it will be on a vastly greater scale. Then the revival will come, along with continued shaking.

THE END-TIME SHAKING WILL IMPACT MULTITUDES ALL OVER THE EARTH; AND, AS PEOPLE TURN TO GOD, THE FINAL REVIVAL WILL COME.

There are few known pockets of revival right now. Several revivals are occurring with our affiliated churches and ministry partners around the world, as well as in other places, but there is not much more going on. Nevertheless, the shaking of all things will bring forth unparalleled revival in coming years.

THE FINAL STAGE

These are the times about which Joel prophesied:

And it shall come to pass afterward that I will pour out My Spirit on all flesh; your sons and your daughters shall prophesy, your old men shall dream dreams, your young men shall see visions. And also on My menservants and on My maidservants I will pour out My Spirit in those days. And I will show wonders in the heavens and in the earth: blood and fire and pillars of smoke. The sun shall be turned into darkness, and the moon into blood, before the coming of the great and awesome day of the LORD. And it shall come to pass that whoever calls on the name of the LORD shall be saved. For in Mount Zion and in Jerusalem there shall be deliverance, as the LORD has said, among the remnant whom the LORD calls. (Joel 2:28–32)

The final shaking with revival will take place before the coming of the Lord. We are living in the concluding days of the feast of Pentecost. The outpouring of the Holy Spirit after Christ's resurrection marked a new era on earth; but, now, we are entering the final stage of that era, which marks the imminent beginning of a new era in the end-time cycle. The return of the Lord is at hand. The last-days outpouring of the Holy Spirit is the final testimony before the coming of Christ.

Again, in this revival, we will see the wonders of God's glory manifested. It will be a sovereign act of God that man's knowledge cannot interpret or resolve. We will see people crying out to the Lord for answers, refuge, and salvation. That's revival—people seeking God in desperation. Then the end will come!

Do you want to participate in the last-days revival? Do you want to be included in the remnant of believers who are sanctified and seek God's presence in prayer? Do you want to be empowered for end-time evangelism?

Do you long for the coming of Christ and the manifestation of His glory? I do! I want revival with all the strength of my being. Every day, I cry out, "Come, Lord Jesus!" I want to see the Holy Spirit being poured out on people in churches, schools, offices, hospitals, prisons, shopping malls, and streets all over the world. I want to see the glory of God in my life and in the lives of my children, both natural and spiritual. I want to see lives changed, hearts transformed and filled with the Spirit of God. If you desire the same, please pray the following prayer with me:

> Lord Jesus, I recognize that there are areas in my life that are not filled with the life of the Holy Spirit. I recognize that my prayer life lacks Your presence. I need an outpouring of Your Spirit. I need to be revived. I recognize that I continue to struggle with certain sins, that there are areas of my life that I have not fully surrendered to You, and that my heart has remained closed and cannot be transformed without the work of Your Spirit. I have felt Your presence, Your touch, and Your love, but I have not yet been transformed by Your power because I have resisted total surrender to You. Today, I repent and ask You to forgive me. I ask You to do a complete work in me. I want to be part of the remnant that seeks Your presence and longs for the end-time revival. In Your name, beloved Jesus, I cry out, "Fill me with the Holy Spirit! Raise me up from this deep sleep and fill my mouth with Your Word! Make me a witness for Christ in my family and in my city!" Amen!

END-TIME TESTIMONIES

Milton and Kristina Martinez are members of King Jesus Ministry in Miami. The doctor who is overseeing Kristina during her pregnancy discovered that the baby she is carrying was missing a chromosome. When Milton and Kristina cried out to the Lord, God worked in a way that the doctors cannot explain. Kristina describes the creative miracle that occurred:

> Three weeks ago, the doctor called to notify us that our baby had a problem with his chromosomes. It was such a serious issue that we immediately knew we had to take refuge under the great I Am.

Together with the elders and mentors of the church, we began to pray and declare healing, covering our baby with the blood of Jesus Christ. The doctors sent me for another test; meanwhile, we tuned in to King Jesus Ministry to participate in an online event called the "Global Day of Prayer and Repentance." The purpose of this forum was to provide an opportunity for believers from all over the world to join together for a full twenty-four hours of intercession and repentance. A few days later, the doctor called with the results and told us that everything was fine. Our baby is 100 percent healthy! God has manifested Himself in a great way, and we are very grateful to Him for all He has done in our lives.

The following is the testimony of a man who had a severe medical condition for which there seemed to be no cure. The doctors had no solution for his pain. In despair, he longed for the Lord to take his life so that he could stop suffering the constant torment of his illness. Then, he came into contact with King Jesus Ministry. As God's remnant, we keep our lamp burning, we preach the gospel of the kingdom, and signs follow us wherever we travel to minister around the world.

My name is Alex, and I'm from New Zealand. I am a member of the worship team at my church, and my daughter and I write songs together. Ever since we attended the Supernatural Encounter that Apostle Guillermo Maldonado hosted in New Zealand, we have been able to see the power of God manifest in our church. However, I was in a hopeless condition before I experienced that power myself. My situation was so extreme that I had even written my obituary and started to put my affairs in order in preparation for departing from this world.

It all started with a toothache. I went to the dentist and had the tooth extracted; however, the pain continued, and I started to have other teeth extracted, including healthy ones. Then, the dentist suspected there might be an underlying medical cause for my pain, so I went to the hospital, where I was finally diagnosed with neuralgia. I went in to the hospital on a Wednesday, and, by Friday, I was in surgery. The medical staff told me everything had gone well and that I would no longer feel pain because they had implanted a Teflon plate to cover the root that was at the base of the nerve so that nothing would ever touch it again. However, after a few hours, the pain returned. I had that pain for ten years. The doctors started giving me ketamine, which is often used as an anesthetic for animals, such as horses. They told me it was the first time they'd had to resort to such an extreme medication for neuralgia.

Due to the intense, ongoing pain, I had no life. I couldn't speak, and I couldn't sleep. I spent day and night in a chair. When my children would greet me in the morning before leaving for the day, I couldn't even open my mouth; I was barely able to emit a grunt in response. If I slept at all, it was because I was exhausted, and I stayed asleep for only a very short time because the pain would come back every three or four minutes. Even after the surgery, I took twelve pills a day. I was living in pain, and I was ready to die. I told my wife, "Now I understand why they call neuralgia the disease of suicide." The idea of dying didn't seem so bad compared to the reality of constant pain.

I took the potent medicine tramadol and other medications, each with its side effects. There was one drug that made my hands shake, but when I attended church, I would take my guitar and play as loudly as I could. The neuralgia never stopped me from worshipping God. Once, I told the Lord that I wanted Him to take me to be with Him, but that I would not stop worshipping Him, no matter what.

Then, I began to hear about Apostle Maldonado's upcoming Supernatural Encounter in Napier, New Zealand. I did not know who Apostle Maldonado was. When people invited me to attend the Encounter, I said that I did not want to go because many people had already prayed for me. However, the truth was that I had already accepted that my life was going to stay the way it was, and that God's grace would be enough. However, I finally decided to go to the Encounter. Before I traveled there, many things happened, including my having such a strong attack of pain that I took as much medicine as I could, thinking I would not be able to endure the trip, but I was able to make it.

When the first service began at the stadium where the Supernatural Encounter was being held, the worship was very powerful; I felt the supernatural power and authority there. God was moving in that stadium—so much so that I could feel His presence over me, lifting all my burdens. A young woman from my church was nearby and started praying for me, and I began to feel relief. It was as if I was waking up from a nightmare. God did great miracles at that Encounter. When I realized I had been healed and could serve Him without any more pain, I felt so much more love for Him. I am so grateful for what God has done in me. Thanks to Him, I will be able to see my five children grow up and get married. My son had been healed of cancer a few years earlier, but now we are living in a new level of God's glory.

I went through ten years of suffering and pain in which I basically had no life—until God healed me! Even if you are going through a dead-end situation, God has a purpose for you beyond what you can imagine. If you need healing, you can be healed now; if you want to be activated in the supernatural, you can be activated now, in the name of Jesus. You just have to be hungry for it. Don't give up! I thought my life was over, but God gave me a second chance. He has shown me that His power is real.

As far as ministry goes, I was disappointed with New Zealand at first because the Encounter wasn't attended by the number of people I thought it would be. In the past, I had been part of a big movement where the stadiums would be completely filled. Now, the supernatural glory is filling the whole earth, and New Zealand is about to enter into that. In fact, a new awakening is beginning. God is creating a movement in His people, and we will see miracles, signs, and wonders. We are happy to have been part of the Supernatural Encounter in New Zealand, and we are ready to see God's promises for our land and the world fulfilled.

CHAPTER 9

WHY REVIVALS DIE OUT

Many of the church denominations that were born as a result of the revivals we surveyed in chapter 7 have lost their fire. In fact, most of the denominations that exist in the world today began in the midst of a great outpouring of the Holy Spirit but, unfortunately, over time, became spiritually lukewarm or dead. They ceased to be houses of God and instead became houses of men. They quenched revival and institutionalized themselves, turning into organizations that appeared to be of God but, in reality, denied His power. *"But know this, that in the last days perilous times will come: for men will…[have] a form of godliness but [deny] its power. And from such people turn away!"* (2 Timothy 3:1–2, 5). The flame that had kept these denominations going in revival went out, and they fell into mindsets and behaviors that were merely natural, rational, entertainment-oriented, and routine. All such characteristics lead to stale ritualism.

WHY HAVE WE LOST REVIVAL?

Most historical revivals have lasted only between eight and ten years because believers have not known how to sustain them. What is often not very clear is *why* this happens. This is the fundamental point we will address in this chapter. If we do not pinpoint the causes of this dilemma, people will continue to repeat the same mistakes because, as the proverbial saying goes, "Those who do not know history are destined to repeat it."

Why do revivals die? In many cases, it is a fulfillment of this prophecy: *"Therefore my people have gone into captivity, because they have no knowledge; their honorable men are famished, and their multitude dried up with thirst"* (Isaiah 5:13). In other cases, revival leaders took certain actions that led to their own downfall, undermining their good work: *"Pride goes before destruction, and a haughty spirit before a fall"* (Proverbs 16:18). One or both of these roots have dragged subsequent generations of believers into one of the following conditions of spiritual decline and lukewarmness.

BEING CRITICAL OF ELEMENTS OF REVIVAL

Almost always, the first blemish that mars a revival is not external criticism by the unconverted (although that often does occur) but rather criticism that comes from within the church itself. *"And if a house is divided against itself, that house cannot stand"* (Mark 3:25). Discernment and wisdom are always essential when dealing with spiritual matters (see, for example, 1 John 4:1), and *"God is not the author of confusion but of peace"* (1 Corinthians 14:33). However, within these Spirit-led guidelines, it is important to allow the Holy Spirit to move as He will and not inhibit His work. Criticism of revival stops the divine move of the Spirit because it perverts it. When revival grows beyond human control, many people begin to censure it. This can negatively affect the leaders of the revival, causing them to doubt themselves so that their convictions concerning the awakening are weakened. Eventually, they are pushed to succumb to the pressure of their critics. It is common for people to criticize what they cannot control or achieve themselves. Therefore, during revival, we must be careful not to yield to undue criticism or to pervert the action of the Spirit among us.

REVIVALS DO NOT END BECAUSE THEY ARE EXCESSIVE; THEY END BECAUSE PEOPLE TRY TO CONTROL THEM.

Additionally, criticism of revivals comes from people who are operating under a carnal mindset. Those who are carnally minded do not know how to discern what is of God, what is of man, and what is of the devil, because their spiritual senses are dull, and they cannot see beyond what they can observe with their natural eyes. Jesus said to His disciples, *"Therefore I speak to them [the multitudes] in parables, because seeing they do not see, and hearing they do not hear, nor do they understand"* (Matthew 13:13). Again, let us not lend our ears to criticism; a mindset of criticism is of the flesh, while a mindset that is discerning and open to God is of the Spirit.

I don't mind being criticized for believing in the supernatural power of God, miracles, or the person of the Holy Spirit rather than in human opinions. The apostle Peter issued this encouragement to believers: *"If you are reproached for the name of Christ, blessed are you, for the Spirit of glory and of God rests upon you"* (1 Peter 4:14). This is the word that sustains me every time criticism arises from the church at large toward my ministry and its demonstrations of supernatural power. Let that same word sustain all of us during the end-time revival.

TO BE BEARERS OF REVIVAL, WE HAVE TO PAY THE GREAT PRICE OF BEING THE RECIPIENTS OF CRITICISM AND GRIEVANCES.

COMPROMISING THE TRUTH

Another reason revivals die out is that, as time passes, it becomes common for leaders of congregations that had previously been living in revival to turn away from the fundamental truth on which the church was built. During the years of revival that followed the outpouring of the Holy Spirit in the upper room, the apostles instructed the believers many times not to depart from the truth. (See, for example, 1 Timothy 4:1–6.) And Jesus warned the church at Ephesus, *"Remember therefore from where you have fallen; repent and do the first works, or else I will come to you quickly and remove your lampstand from its place—unless you repent"* (Revelation 2:5). When we compromise the truth, God removes His presence and His Spirit from our midst. The apostles understood this reality. That's why they were zealous to prevent the outpouring of God's Spirit from being quenched.

During the various revivals that have occurred over the centuries since the early church, many preachers have compromised the truth for the sake of gaining prestige, fame, position, money, or pleasure. Others have compromised the truth because they lacked a clear identity in Christ and were not established in the truth. Still others have done so for the sake of following other people's opinions, to secure favorable public opinion for themselves, to please others, and so on. What they did not take into account was that God's judgment for compromising the truth is always the removal of one's lampstand from its place and the withdrawal of the Holy Spirit and His presence. People pay a high price for giving in to spiritual deception and self-serving pursuits. Even now, because they compromised the truth, many people are in hell, while, for the same reason, some Christians will not be taken by Christ in the rapture but will be left on earth during the tribulation.

REJECTING THE WORK OF THE HOLY SPIRIT

As incredible as it may seem, this may be the most common sin in the church today. Churches reject the work of the Holy Spirit in order to keep to a predetermined schedule, to preserve "order," and to satisfy those who do not feel comfortable with demonstrations of the Spirit. Therefore, when the Spirit manifests during a service, many preachers do not grant Him His rightful place and authority. There are even some ministers who are unable to discern what does and does not come from the Holy Spirit. Thus, the Spirit of God is quenched and grieved in the church, even though the Bible clearly commands us not to allow this to happen. (See, for example, 1 Thessalonians 5:19; Ephesians 4:30.) If the Holy Spirit pulls away from a church, that church automatically becomes a human-directed congregation where people live with evil spirits, such as those of religiosity, manipulation, and lying. That is a dangerous situation because, outwardly, the church may appear to be a house of God, even though God's Holy Spirit no longer dwells there. This opens the door to even more spiritual deception and transgressions.

THE GREATEST CONSEQUENCE OF REJECTING THE HOLY SPIRIT IS SPIRITUAL DEATH. THAT IS THE DANGER OF EMBRACING THE BELIEFS OF THOSE WHO ARE SPIRITUALLY DRY OR DEAD.

LACKING SPIRITUAL FATHERS

Every generation that has participated in revival has been led by believers who have assumed the role of spiritual father—interceding for, nurturing, and perpetuating the movement of the Spirit. These leaders have watched, prayed, fasted, and otherwise paid the price to receive the revival. The sad thing is that when the first generation of leaders passes, the revival tends to die out because the leaders did not know how to properly train the next generation in the knowledge and practice of the supernatural power that was imparted to them by the Spirit. Today, even with so many advancements and resources available to us, whether materially or virtually through the Internet—including Bible schools, manuals, training platforms, Christian books, and so forth—we still do not have many "schools of the Spirit" training people in the supernatural and teaching believers how to sustain revivals or continue the legacy of spiritual renewal in their cities and nations.

Why is this the case? There are two reasons. First, for a long time, the church has rejected the biblical ministry of the apostle. (See Ephesians 4:11–12.) However, the apostles are the spiritual fathers whom God raises up to transfer spiritual inheritance to new generations. The second reason is a consequence of the first. Without spiritual fathers, believers in the next generation have no one to invest in them to continue the revival. No one trains them or passes along revelation to them; they are left as spiritual orphans! As a result, each generation has to start from scratch, with certain believers paying the price of praying for revival and learning from their own mistakes and failures until they attain the promise of the Spirit's outpouring and become the fathers of a new supernatural movement.

And that is the best-case scenario. At other times, it takes several generations before new leaders are raised up to call for revival and rekindle the flame of the Spirit. And, still, no one seems able to leave a revival legacy for the next generation. The apostle Paul is the best example of a true spiritual father. He left not just one but many legacies of his walk with Christ. With ample reason, he expressed to the believers in Corinth, *"For though you might have ten thousand instructors in Christ, yet you do not have many fathers; for in Christ Jesus I have begotten you through the gospel"* (1 Corinthians 4:15).

So, what is a major reason for the lack of spiritual fathers? It is that the church has not only misunderstood the process that leads to revival, but it has also made a doctrine out of that misunderstanding! According to many Christians, past revivals came to revitalize the church but were never meant to continue longer than they did. Such a mindset implies that revivals last a specific length of time, and then they stop, allowing us to return to "normal" Christianity, where we wait for the next initiative of the Holy Spirit to arrive. It is clear that these Christians have no revelation of fatherhood or spiritual heritage. It's as if we have to be content with living from visitation to visitation of the Spirit. This is not what God wants! He wants us to make room for Him to dwell among us always.

Revival should be a Christian lifestyle, leading us to live "*from glory to glory*" (2 Corinthians 3:18). Remember the words of Haggai: "'*The glory of this latter temple shall be greater than the former,*' says the LORD *of hosts. 'And in this place, I will give peace,*' says the LORD *of hosts*" (Haggai 2:9). The next generation should be even greater in power and glory than its predecessor—and the subsequent generation even more so, until the earth is completely filled with the glory of God. (See Habakkuk 2:14.)

As a spiritual father, my duty is to lead our current generation to experience the end-time revival. I owe this generation an encounter with the supernatural power of God! On the cross, Jesus paid the price for all our sins. Salvation is free for us, but it cost Him His life; He paid for it with His blood. It is my responsibility to show the world how to value the work of the cross, how to cherish the gift of salvation, and how to pay the price of revival.

This is one of my challenges and functions as an apostle. I have to build a bridge for people to enter the end-time revival with revelation, and to help their natural and spiritual children to continue to fan the flame so that it keeps growing—transforming individuals and societies. When the goal is to see a generation awaken to revival, any sacrifice is worth it! It was God's desire that revival be followed through from the beginning of the era of the Holy Spirit at Pentecost to the end of that era when Christ returns.

Just as with natural children, our spiritual children must be carried on our shoulders at first until they learn to walk and then run. They are called to inherit what we have achieved, carry it forward, grow it, and expand it. Tragically, the present generation is a generation without fathers; that is why the earth is filled with spiritual orphans. And that is why one of my roles as an apostle is to give spiritual fatherhood to others and to impart a legacy to this generation. These are the true marks of an apostle. Many people want the title and prestige of being called "apostle" but do not want to accept the responsibilities, experience the hurts, make the sacrifices, or endure the hard work involved in being a Christlike apostle. The proclamation of the gospel has been delayed twenty, thirty, and even fifty years in certain countries of the world due to a lack of spiritual fatherhood.

I don't believe the legacy of revival has passed from one generation to the next for the last two hundred years! Again, most revivals have lasted eight to ten years before dying out for various reasons, some of which we have already discussed, including a lack of spiritual fathers who are meant to pass on the revival legacy. Sadly, as we have seen, this scenario became a pattern. The first generation of Christians was immersed in a powerful revival, but when the second generation came onto the scene, the revival died out almost immediately. By the time the third generation came around, the revival was forgotten. The church became nothing more than an organization that was attractive to the masses; Christianity was left to be developed by people who shared mere human relationships and goals. Thus, the movement and manifestations of the Holy Spirit were allowed to diminish until people were left solely with formulas, rituals, religious brotherhoods, denominations, and institutions where there were activities but not the presence of the one true God, where people were entertained but their lives were not transformed. This is the case with our generation today. Many mighty "generals" of recent past revivals have departed to be with the Lord—Oral Roberts, Kenneth Hagin, and T. L. Osborn, among others—and their movements have departed with them.

What should we learn from all this? We must be critically aware that we have to pass along a legacy to our spiritual children so they can keep the movement of the Spirit alive and take it to more people, more cities, and more nations. Again, my assignment as a spiritual father is to enable this generation to experience the ultimate revival—and to teach them the price they will need to pay in order to do so.

IF SPIRITUAL FATHERS ARE INVESTED IN THE NEXT GENERATION, REVIVAL WILL REMAIN AND BE MAINTAINED.

BEING DECEIVED BY END-TIME APOSTASY

Today, before our very eyes, we are seeing the end-time apostasy that was prophesied about in the Bible. Millions of people are turning away from their faith in Christ. The number of people who attend church is decreasing because of the apostasy that is sweeping the earth. *"The Spirit expressly says that in latter times some will depart from the faith, giving heed to deceiving spirits and doctrines of demons, speaking lies in hypocrisy, having their own conscience seared"* (1 Timothy 4:1–2). This is happening now! There are people who, having once been believers, now openly deny Christ. They have become enemies of God, denying Jesus's finished work on the cross and His resurrection, and grieving and quenching the Holy Spirit and His supernatural power. They do not believe in the rapture or the second coming of Christ, and they either twist the truth or directly deny it.

> *Now, brethren, concerning the coming of our Lord Jesus Christ and our gathering together to Him, we ask you,…let no one deceive you by any means; for that Day will not come unless the falling away comes first, and the man of sin is revealed, the son of perdition.*
> (2 Thessalonians 2:1, 3)

As we have discussed, this era of apostasy has given birth to a church that accommodates those who compromise the truth for fear of offending people. In order to keep people from dropping out of church or going to another congregation, many churches do not hesitate to compromise their fundamental principles—even if it means becoming a church that is merely comfortable and fun for people to attend, that soothes people's emotions but leaves them free to remain in their sin, that does not tell them what displeases the Lord and fails to teach them how God wants to transform their hearts. That kind of church accepts mankind's rebellion, sin, pride, and lust. This is how many congregations retain their membership nowadays.

THE SPIRIT OF APOSTASY HAS CAUSED A DIVISION IN THE BODY OF CHRIST: IT HAS PLACED THE SUPERNATURAL CHURCH ON ONE SIDE AND THE "SEEKER-FRIENDLY" CHURCH ON THE OTHER.

It is time for the remnant bride to cry out for revival so that the church of Christ may awaken from its deep sleep, repent, renounce the spirit of deception, and receive *"times of refreshing"* (Acts 3:19) from the Lord. Although the increasing influence of a spirit of apostasy is predicted in biblical end-time prophecy, we can pray for Christians to come out of their spiritual slumber and indifference and be reignited with holy fire for Christ.

MAKE ROOM FOR THE SPIRIT

In this chapter, we have learned the main reasons why revivals end: the church criticizes elements of revival; it compromises the truth; it rejects the work of the Holy Spirit; it lacks spiritual fathers; and it allows itself to be deceived by end-time apostasy. Now that we know all this, how should we respond? We can correct these errors so that revival can return. If we do not do this, we will experience the following consequences: the presence of God will leave (or not return to) our midst; we will enter into spiritual darkness; the next generation will have to start from scratch to see revival; the church will lack spiritual fathers; and the spirit of apostasy will continue to deceive the children of God. We cannot allow this to happen! We must allow the zeal of the Lord to move us to stand up and be the voice of God's truth on earth, to denounce what is wrong and give room to the Holy Spirit to pour out His fire and bring the last and greatest revival this earth has ever seen!

END-TIME TESTIMONIES

A sixteen-year-old girl named Jael was transformed by God through my book *Breakthrough Prayer*. She experienced the power of the Holy Spirit to change lives. Today, she sees His power daily in the Argentinian ministry of her parents, Diego and Roxana, who are under the covering of King Jesus Ministry.

My name is Jael, and I belong to a church in Argentina, founded by my parents, called Ministerio Herederos de la Promesa (Heirs of the Promise Ministry). Since my family and I started doing God's work in this church, I have been able to experience God's power as a youth leader in my nation. It all started when I received the book *Breakthrough Prayer*. I had a relationship with God previously, but it wasn't an intimate or everyday relationship. After reading this book, though, I began to understand who God is. I started to respect His presence and get to truly know Him. The more I read, the more my desire to pray increased. I began to pray more intimately, and God began to give me deep revelation about His Word. No one prayed for me to experience these things, but no one needed to. It was the Holy Spirit who baptized me and led me to repent and change my relationship with God and with other people. I started to relate to others, to have love and compassion for them.

Our ministry has seen lives impacted, and we have grown. We have seen end-time revival during this difficult crisis [the coronavirus pandemic]. God's people are manifesting, and we are seeing the movement of the remnant. We are seeing powerful financial miracles! In just three weeks, we have seen three hundred souls won through our online services, even in the midst of the quarantine.

I would like to share the testimony of a twenty-one-year-old man who, as a child, was forced to be part of a gang of drug dealers and robbers that his parents belonged to. He suffered much abuse there but was able to escape this influence and be set free through our ministry.

My name is Matias. I lived in Buenos Aires, and my family belonged to a group of robbers, drug dealers, and murderers. During my childhood, I saw horrible things. My father was stabbed to death next to me. I saw other people get shot to death, including a baby girl. My mom used me to go out and steal for her. But I was very young, and I didn't want to steal, so I stayed at street corners where there were traffic lights and begged people for money instead. One day, some people saw me and told my mom what I was doing. To punish me, they locked me in a very dirty bathroom with no lights. There, two men beat me, stabbed me, and broke my teeth. As a child, I suffered a lot of abuse: my mom would bang my head against the wall so much that it became difficult for me to speak. I didn't want nighttime to come because I knew the beatings would be even worse. No one would talk to me or tell me anything. I soon became an addict, taking pills and drugs. Finally, there came a time when I knew I didn't want to live this kind of life anymore. Then, some friends from Olavarria (a city far from there) looked for me and took me away from that situation. They told me that I would be able to finish school. I was in treatment for a year in Olavarria. Once I got better, I wanted to look for the people who had hurt me and get revenge, but God was always there with me, preventing that from happening.

One day, I was sitting in front of a river, wanting to kill myself, when I heard a voice telling me, "You have a purpose." Thank God, today, I am alive, and I am able to speak, despite my earlier injury. Additionally, I was told I would become blind, but I can see.

I came to know about God through a man who took me to a House of Peace meeting. I was still full of fear, though, and I ran away from there. But the man didn't give up. He spoke to me again and took me to church. Now, I follow God. I serve as an usher, and I know my purpose. My life was hard, but God changed it. Here I have found a real family and spiritual parents. They helped me and gave me advice; they were my primary examples as parents. I could never call my natural parents "Dad" and "Mom," but I could do that with these people. I was able to forgive my biological family. I experienced what it is like to have true friendships. God never left me alone. He did not reject me or abandon me. He gave me strength, peace, and a love that I had never experienced before.

Nuria Serrano is a young woman who, after experiencing God's love, left our church and returned to her old life in the world. Ten years later, her life was under great spiritual attack, especially in her mental health. God's intervention saved her and revived what was dead inside her. He brought her back into His presence and into an intimate relationship with Him.

Ten years ago, I served as an elder at King Jesus Ministry, but my parents' divorce and other family problems contributed to a lack of healing in my emotions. My relationship with God began to cool down because I didn't dedicate the necessary time to it, even though I spent many hours serving in the church. One thing led to another, but it wasn't until I had a disagreement with my mentor that I decided to leave the church. Many things happened after that, but, at the beginning of last year, everything I had not dealt with in God's presence began to be reflected in my physical health. I started to suffer panic attacks and anxiety. I couldn't work, I couldn't drive my car, and I had to sleep with someone else in the room because I couldn't handle my emotions. I began to have thoughts of suicide and ended up in a psychiatric hospital against my will, due to a mandate under the Baker Act.[98]

While I was in the waiting room of the hospital, I looked around and felt that I did not belong there. So, I closed my eyes and said, "God, You are all I have. There's no one here but You and me. Get me out of here." At that moment, I knew I had to return to God. An hour later, the doctors told me, "You don't belong here. Call

---

98. The Baker Act is a Florida law that allows family members and loved ones to request emergency mental health services and temporary detention for people who are disabled due to mental illness and who cannot determine their own treatment needs.

someone to come and get you." Still confused and not understanding how I had ended up there, what was going on, or where those thoughts were coming from, I called my boss at work. He brought me home and told me, "You have to go back to the church." I knew that God was calling me back there, so I called one of my former disciples, and he invited me to a deliverance retreat. From that day forward, my life has not been the same. Everything has changed. I have been able to see God move in my life in a new way. I am so happy! And I know that I will see His promises fulfilled. I know that what God has for me is wonderful. Even though I didn't understand what was happening, God had everything planned out. He turned everything that was bad in my life into a process that led me back into His presence. Now I can serve Him and see His promises fulfilled. He produced a revival within me, and now I can see His glory every day.

CHAPTER 10

THE PURPOSE OF REVIVAL

We are living in a time of restoration. God is reestablishing many truths and principles in the church so we can experience the spiritual realities that were part of His original intention for humanity. The first of these renewals is the restoration of His presence in our lives. God's original intention was that human beings would permanently dwell in His presence. He doesn't want to just "visit" us from time to time; He longs to *live among us*. That is why, in these end times, we will see unusual manifestations of God's presence that will restore humanity to the place of privilege that our heavenly Father assigned to us. To be in God's presence is like being face-to-face with Him. Today, He calls us to repentance that will bring us back to that wonderful place of being in His presence.

> *Repent therefore and be converted, that your sins may be blotted out,* ***so that times of refreshing may come from the presence of the Lord,*** *and that He may send Jesus Christ, who was preached to you before, whom heaven must receive **until the times of restoration of all things,** which God has spoken by the mouth of all His holy prophets since the world began.* (Acts 3:19–21)

When the people of Israel journeyed in the desert on their way to the promised land, God's presence was continually with them, manifested in the pillar of cloud by day and the pillar of fire by night. (See, for example, Exodus 13:21–22.) However, the Israelites took God's continual presence with them for granted, not valuing His closeness to them. The same thing is happening in the church today. We have taken God's presence lightly and have even abused His purposes for us by focusing on obtaining personal benefits from Him instead of seeking His presence and allowing ourselves to be transformed into the image and likeness of our Creator.

REVIVAL COMES TO AWAKEN AND RESTORE PEOPLE'S HEARTS TO GOD.

There is a similar attitude among some people in the church who believe that the purpose of revival is to "have a good time" or to merely have emotional experiences—to laugh, to cry, to dance, to fall down, or to roll on the floor. They confuse revival with entertainment, which satisfies the natural senses and desires of the flesh but does not, in itself, bring about transformation. Such attitudes are another reason most revivals never reach their full potential and tend to fade away after eight or ten years.

Being in God's presence implies being transformed. When people have been truly changed, their transformation will be evident to those around them by their new outlook and behavior. Sometimes, there may even be a tangible sign that a believer has been in the presence of God. The most prominent biblical example is when Moses's face glowed after he had been with the Lord on Mount Sinai:

> *Now it was so, when Moses came down from Mount Sinai (and the two tablets of the Testimony were in Moses' hand when he came down from the mountain), that Moses did not know that the skin of his face shone while he talked with Him. So when Aaron and all the children of Israel saw Moses, behold, the skin of his face shone, and they were afraid to come near him.* (Exodus 34:29–30)

GOD'S PURPOSES IN REVIVAL

To understand why God brings revival, let's begin by reviewing the meaning of *purpose* in relation to a person or an object. Generally, *purpose* refers to the fundamental reason for which something was created. One dictionary definition of *purpose* is "something set up as an object or end to be attained."[99] In a biblical context, the purpose of creation is God's original intention for making all things on earth and giving life to mankind. Like everything God does, revival has definite and specific purposes. Let's explore several of these purposes.

TO RESTORE MANKIND TO GOD'S PRESENCE

Mankind was meant to live in God's presence and to experience His manifest glory. The manifest glory of God is the expression of His love, holiness, and sovereignty. As we read in Genesis, mankind's life began in the presence of God. His life and presence were the foundation and nourishment of humanity's very existence. But when human beings disobeyed God by eating fruit from the Tree of Knowledge of Good and Evil, which He had instructed them not to do, the first thing they did was flee from God's presence and hide from Him. *"And they heard the sound of the* LORD *God walking in the garden in the cool of the day, and Adam and his wife* **hid themselves from the presence of the** LORD **God** *among the trees of the garden"* (Genesis 3:8).

Before Adam and Eve fell, their whole life was filled with God's presence. *"You will show me the path of life; in Your presence is fullness of joy; at Your right hand are pleasures forevermore"* (Psalm 16:11). When they sinned, they lost everything of true value. As long as they remained in the presence of God, human beings had everything. But outside of that presence, they had nothing. They became incomplete, deformed, and empty. Therefore, it is not surprising to see that, without God, people today live their lives trying to find fulfillment from other sources. Some people become fully devoted to work; others pursue sports, entertainment, or sexual pleasure; still others fall into drugs, crime, or other vices; and so on. Through various avenues, people seek to fill the void in their inner being, which can only be filled by the presence of God. Jesus gave His life on the cross, overcame

---

99. *Merriam-Webster.com Dictionary*, s.v. "purpose," https://www.merriam-webster.com/dictionary/purpose.

death, and rose again so that our relationship with the Father might be restored, so that we might again have access to the glorious, life-giving presence of God.

After the fall of mankind, the Father promised that Jesus would come to redeem human beings so they would not have to live outside His presence forever. (See Genesis 3:15.) He longs for us to be restored to Him. The fundamental reason He created human beings was to have communion and fellowship with them.

IN ORDER TO BELIEVE IN SOMETHING, YOU MUST KNOW ITS PURPOSE.

Jesus's coming to earth as a human being to be our Savior is written about in both the Old and New Testaments, including the following verses: *"Therefore the Lord Himself will give you a sign: Behold, the virgin shall conceive and bear a Son, and shall call His name Immanuel"* (Isaiah 7:14). *"'Behold, the virgin shall be with child, and bear a Son, and they shall call His name Immanuel,' which is translated, 'God with us'"* (Matthew 1:23). The Lord came to redeem us from our sins so that He could dwell among us again: *"And what agreement has the temple of God with idols? For you are the temple of the living God. As God has said: 'I will dwell in them and walk among them. I will be their God, and they shall be My people'"* (2 Corinthians 6:16).

Thus, the purpose of the total restoration of God's presence in our lives is for Him, as Immanuel, to live with His children. At the end of the book of Revelation we read, *"Behold, the tabernacle of God is with men, and He will dwell with them, and they shall be His people. God Himself will be with them and be their God"* (Revelation 21:3).

Our salvation in Jesus restores us to living in God's presence—our original purpose. This purpose of living in His presence is above any other callings, ministries, or gifts we have received. Only as we live in His presence can we fulfill these callings, ministries, and gifts in a proper, healthy, and fruitful way.

God does not want our "religion." Neither does He want us to exercise spiritual power outside the context of our relationship with Him. He does not desire people who claim to have faith in Him but do not dwell with Him. God desires to have a relationship with the people He has lovingly created in His image. When we are restored to His presence and dwell with Him, revival will come!

In the realm of the supernatural, there are three dimensions: faith, anointing, and glory. Living in each of these dimensions is a distinct experience. To live by faith is to live by principle; to live by anointing is to live by the power of God; but to live by glory is to live in God's presence. Living in the dimension of glory means having a close and intimate relationship with the Lord—the original Source of all power and the principles that sustain it. Living by faith demands work, but living in God's presence enables us to rest in Him as He does the work. While we rest in Him, miracles spring from that intimacy.

THE PERSON WHO HAS NOT BEEN RESTORED TO THE PRESENCE OF GOD PRACTICES MERE RELIGIOUS ROUTINES AND RITES.

Our faith is measured by what we know and do, but God's presence cannot be measured because it is subject to His sovereignty. Living by faith and anointing is important, but living in God's presence is vital. For a Christian, living in God's presence is a matter of life and death. If we do not live in His presence, we will not be able to leave with Christ when He raptures His church. Only when God's presence is restored in an individual or in a congregation will true revival come.

God's chosen people, the Israelites, for whom He worked many of the greatest wonders and miracles in history, lost the presence of God Almighty, or *El Shaddai*, one of the names by which He was known among the patriarchs. The Israelites were in a battle against the Philistines, and the Philistines captured the ark of the covenant, which is where God would manifest His presence. The Philistines also killed the two sons of Eli the priest. When Eli heard this terrible news, he fell backward and died. His daughter-in-law went into premature labor and named her newborn son *Ichabod*, which means "inglorious." Before she died, she said, *"The glory has departed from Israel, for the ark of God has been captured"* (1 Samuel 4:22).

ALL REVIVAL BEGINS WITH THE RESTORATION OF MAN TO THE PRESENCE OF GOD.

Similarly, God's presence is absent from many churches today. What does a church look like without the presence of the Lord? Everything might seem right and in order there, and the church might appear to be functioning well—yet, in reality, it is impersonal, spiritually powerless, dry, dead. It is inclined toward the natural rather than the supernatural, toward entertainment and motivational messages rather than the Word of God. The fact is, where there is no presence of God, people accept a religion of formulas, methods, and rituals; they are content with rational and human methods alone, without realizing they are missing what is most important.

Furthermore, there are Christians who believe that God's presence will come if they sing certain songs, preach in a certain way or on a certain theme, or cry and shout. Others think that a full congregation indicates the presence of God. They focus on outward appearances rather than seeking His genuine presence. In this way, they engage in dead works, hoping to experience the life of God in their own way. However, when we truly seek the living God, we come to understand that methods and formulas do not work. We learn that we need revelation in order to be restored to His presence. Until we understand and act on this truth, we will not have a genuine church. We may have a club, an organization, or even a religious institution, but not a church. We will not have the life of the Spirit. That is why the end times will bring about an all-inclusive revival. Then, nothing will be lacking because the presence of God will bring prosperity, joy, peace, miracles, health, transformation, rest, and much more. Everything from God will be present and visible to everyone.

GOD'S PRESENCE IS THE REALM OF TOTAL PROVISION.

TO TRANSFORM SOCIETY

In the modern church, there is much teaching and preaching. However, revival is not widespread because most of this teaching and preaching is directed to the mind, not the heart. Faith is considered to be a mental exercise that does not involve the heart. However, the ministry of Jesus Christ on earth was that of liberating the oppressed and healing the brokenhearted:

> *The Spirit of the* Lord *is upon Me, because He has anointed Me to preach the gospel to the poor; He has sent Me to heal the brokenhearted, to proclaim liberty to the captives and recovery of sight to the blind, to set at liberty those who are oppressed; to proclaim the acceptable year of the* Lord. (Luke 4:18–19)

If a person's heart is not touched by the presence of God, it will remain hardened, and that person will not change.

REVIVAL THAT CHANGES THE HEART BRINGS RESTORATION, TRANSFORMATION, AND REFORMATION TO SOCIETY AS A WHOLE.

Every revival that has impacted the earth has amazed people, not only by the supernatural signs it has brought, but also by the transformation it has caused in the hearts of individuals. The behavior of those who previously lived without God and without hope begins to change. These individuals no longer engage in blasphemy, obscene language, lies, drunkenness, immorality, bitterness, anger, dishonesty, selfishness, or other transgressions. For example, the Pensacola Revival in the mid- to late 1990s was a revival of the presence of God that dealt with the heart; as a result, it had worldwide impact. If any revival falls short in results, it is because people do not yield their hearts to be changed.

Today, the "ark of the covenant," or God's presence, resides within believers. His presence no longer dwells in a physical tabernacle or temple but in the hearts of each of us. (See, for example, 1 Corinthians 3:16.) The great need today is for the tabernacle of our hearts to be purified. In revival, the Lord works in our hearts to transform our character; He cleanses our motives and intentions. This transformation is not a passing emotion; it is a radical and complete life change. When we recognize that there are still parts of our being that we need to surrender to God, we spontaneously begin to humble ourselves before His presence. *"If My people who are called by My name will humble themselves, and pray and seek My face, and turn from their wicked ways, then I will hear from heaven, and will forgive their sin and heal their land"* (2 Chronicles 7:14). As God's people humble their hearts before Him and are transformed in His presence, such transformation cannot go unnoticed by the rest of society.

END-TIME REVIVAL BEGINS IN THE HEART, WHERE GOD'S PRESENCE RESTS AND BRINGS TRANSFORMATION TO THE LIVES OF INDIVIDUALS, WHO CAN THEN TRANSFORM COMMUNITIES AND NATIONS.

We know that this generation will witness the great revival that is about to shake the earth. This awakening will radically change society because it will begin in people's hearts. It will address the brokenness people will be experiencing after the shaking of all things. It will go beyond the four walls of the church and spread to people we might never have expected could be reached. God will reveal Himself to people in unusual places. Remember how Christ revealed Himself to Paul when he was on his way to Damascus to continue arresting and killing Christians, and how Paul's life was radically changed? (See Acts 9:1–22; 26:4–23.) And remember how Philip, led by the Spirit, explained the gospel to the

Ethiopian eunuch who was reading the Scriptures as he traveled along the road from Jerusalem to Gaza? It was the Lord Himself who touched the eunuch's heart and made him desire to be baptized in water as a sign of his new life in Christ. (See Acts 8:26–39.)

Today, God is directly reaching out to people in His sovereignty. We are hearing about unusual encounters in which the Lord is appearing to Muslims in dreams and visions. For example, Ibn Yakoobi and other Muslim extremists in central Africa attacked Christians who were praying at a church. They destroyed the church building and attempted to kill the pastor but were unsuccessful because God protected His people in a dramatic way. After witnessing God's supernatural protection, Ibn was full of questions, but when he challenged local Muslim leaders about their opposition to the Christians, they severely beat him. Lying on the ground with broken bones, Ibn saw a vision of Jesus, who told him, "You are healed by My wounds. You are purified by My blood. You have salvation by My death. And you have eternal life by My resurrection. Now I give you a new heart and new life. Be faithful." Ibn believed in Christ, and he and some of the other attackers who became Christians asked the church members for forgiveness and helped to rebuild their church building.[100]

REVIVAL BEGINS WITHIN PEOPLE AS THEY RESPOND TO THE PROMPTING OF THE HOLY SPIRIT; THEN, THE OUTPOURING OF THE GLORY COMES FROM HEAVEN TO EARTH AS A SOVEREIGN WORK OF GOD.

This great revival will not come from a particular leader, because the Holy Spirit will revive the heart of each person. One individual whose heart has been transformed will stir up the transformation of a family; that family will transform a city; that city will transform a nation; and

100. Minoo Hussain, "God Restores and Redeems: An Astounding Update of Attack on the African Church," Bibles for Mideast, March 19, 2017, https://www.bibles4mideast.com/home-1/2017/03/19/god-restores-and-redeems-an-astounding-update-of-attack-on-the-african-church.

that nation will transform other nations. All this transformation will accumulate, and when the revival is at its peak, there will be a spontaneous outpouring of God's glory. *"Come, and let us return to the LORD; for He has torn, but He will heal us; He has stricken, but He will bind us up. After two days He will revive us; on the third day He will raise us up, that we may live in His sight"* (Hosea 6:1–2).

There are Christians who have supernatural experiences when they go to God's house, but when they return home, their lives remain the same. They have a momentary, circumstantial encounter, yet nothing transformational occurs. They may feel God's presence—because He is real and makes Himself known—but they do not yield their hearts to receive Him. Some people are dead inside, so they focus on what is external; they respond to stimuli but do not receive life, so they do not change. If we want to see our society transformed, we must allow the anointing of the Holy Spirit to penetrate our hearts, because that is where true change takes place. We ourselves must be transformed in God's presence to bring revival to others in the church. Then, revival will spread everywhere, transforming society!

IT IS NOT ENOUGH TO BE TOUCHED BY GOD'S PRESENCE. WE MUST BE TRANSFORMED SO THAT REVIVAL REACHES ALL OF SOCIETY.

TO CLEANSE THE BRIDE OF ALL CONTAMINATION

Christ...loved the church and gave Himself for her, that He might sanctify and cleanse her with the washing of water by the word, that He might present her to Himself a glorious church, not having spot or wrinkle or any such thing, but that she should be holy and without blemish. (Ephesians 5:25–27)

Revival is always related to what Christ wants to do for His bride. In this last-days revival, more than ever, Jesus's purpose is to prepare the church for His coming. As described in part I of this book, shaking comes to remove from the church everything that does not please God. After the shaking comes revival that purifies people's hearts from all uncleanness so that they will finally be transformed.

JESUS IS COMING FOR A GLORIOUS, HOLY, UNBLEMISHED, UNPOLLUTED CHURCH.

If you long for the coming of the Son of God, you must cleanse your life of all defilement, both of the flesh and of the spirit. (See 2 Corinthians 7:1.) There can be no sinfulness or mingling of spirits. There cannot be a little bit of God and a little bit of the flesh, a little bit of holiness and a little bit of sin. In short, we must see revival as God's provision for us to be purified so that we will not miss the rapture.

TO RESTORE MANKIND TO ITS RELATIONSHIP WITH GOD

Earlier, we saw that the chief purpose of revival is to restore mankind to God's presence. That restoration occurs when the church is brought back into relationship with the Creator. To help us understand this truth better, we can divide the work of the Holy Spirit in people's lives into two stages. The first stage leads people to be born again, to have a new life in Christ, which initiates an intimate and personal relationship with the Father. The second stage consists of the transformation of people's hearts, which culminates when the life of God fully dwells in them. If their hearts are not changed, it will be difficult to restore their relationships with the Father.

Today, in much of the church, people's relationships with God are waning; they lack close fellowship with Him. That is why revival is so necessary. Everything that Jesus did on earth as a Man was because of His relationship with the Father through the Holy Spirit. (See, for example, John 5:19.) As children of God, we have been given the same relationship with the Father that Jesus had through His Holy Spirit, who was sent to us for this purpose after Christ ascended to the Father.

Relationship is what draws God to us; through that fellowship, He reveals His presence. The Father is looking for transparent people who want to have a deep, intimate relationship with Him. Human beings were designed to have communion with their Creator. *"But the hour is coming, and now is, when the true worshipers will worship the Father in spirit and truth; for the Father is seeking such to worship Him"* (John 4:23). This is the restoration that will be brought about by the end-time revival: men and women with transformed, pure, undefiled hearts will worship the Father *"in spirit and truth."* When this occurs, the return of Jesus will be imminent.

RELATIONSHIP WITH GOD IS A CONDITION FOR LIVING IN HIS PRESENCE.

A relationship with God is not automatic or instantaneous; it is something we must work at and invest time in, putting the "self" to death every day. This relationship comes about through prayer and develops through persistence in prayer. Through prayer, we come to know the heart of God and gradually grow closer to Him. Jesus related intimately to the Father through prayer because prayer is nothing more than communication between two people who love each other. Deep down, those who do not like prayer are saying that they do not accept the life commitment involved in maintaining their relationship with their heavenly Father. They don't pursue the relationship because they don't want to spend time praying (getting to know Him) and seeking that intimacy. Those who seek God in prayer are more sensitive to God's presence and respond more quickly to it because their hearts are surrendered to Him and to maintaining their relationship with Him. Where there is no relationship, people are cold and insensitive to spiritual matters, and they are unwilling to receive God's presence. Revival reveals the true state of our relationship with the Father and brings about a realignment in our prayer life. Only repentance will cause our hearts to turn to prayer.

OUR DAILY RELATIONSHIP WITH GOD IS ENHANCED THROUGH PRAYER. AS A RESULT, WE BEGIN TO BEAR NEW FRUIT AND RECEIVE ANSWERS TO OUR REQUESTS.

When the church is in revival, prayer meetings become powerful; people have a renewed spiritual passion and an intense desire to be in God's presence. In contrast, as we have been discussing, when people are not right before the Lord, they have no desire to seek the Father's presence. That is what happened to Adam and Eve in the garden of Eden after they disobeyed God. The evidence that we are in revival is that we have a present, strong, intimate, continuing, and growing relationship with the Lord. Moreover, the weight of His presence in us is linked to the intensity and validity of our relationship with Him.

When we are right before God, justified by faith in Christ, we feel comfortable in His presence, and we do not want to depart from Him. We want to pray and worship all the time, because prayer and worship cause God's presence in our lives to be continual, not occasional. As I expressed earlier, when this happens, God does not just "visit" us; God dwells fully in us and with us. In Hebrew, worship is understood as an act of intimacy; it means coming face-to-face with God. Indeed, there is no part of the human body that can more genuinely express a total sense of intimacy than a person's face. When we run away from someone, when there is no intimacy with them, we cannot look them in the eye.

THE EVIDENCE OF OUR RELATIONSHIP WITH GOD IS THAT WE ARE REVIVED BY HIS SPIRIT.

It is out of a close relationship with God that our desire to please and serve Him is born. We readily obey His commands. When we say to the Lord, *"Here am I! Send me"* (Isaiah 6:8), we are really affirming our commitment to Him. If we do not obey God, we have no real relationship with

Him because we cannot love Him without serving Him, and we cannot faithfully serve Him without loving Him. (See John 14:15; Luke 16:13; 10:27.) Jesus expressed this idea clearly when His disciples asked Him how He would manifest Himself to them after He returned to heaven: *"If anyone loves Me, he will keep My word; and My Father will love him, and We will come to him and make Our home with him"* (John 14:23).

OUR PRAYER, WORSHIP, AND OBEDIENCE TO GOD DEMONSTRATE THAT WE KNOW HIM.

TO EMPOWER BELIEVERS FOR THE HARVEST

Then I looked, and behold, a white cloud, and on the cloud sat One like the Son of Man, having on His head a golden crown, and in His hand a sharp sickle. And another angel came out of the temple, crying with a loud voice to Him who sat on the cloud, "Thrust in Your sickle and reap, for the time has come for You to reap, for the harvest of the earth is ripe." (Revelation 14:14–15)

The final purpose of revival is to empower believers to reap the end-time harvest. Once more, in these end times, we will witness the greatest harvest of souls the church has ever seen! People will turn to God because of the shaking of all earthly and temporal things. Therefore, one of the marks of the end-time revival will be a great mobilization of people who are willing to win souls. *"Do you not say, 'There are still four months and then comes the harvest'? Behold, I say to you, lift up your eyes and look at the fields, for they are already white for harvest!"* (John 4:35).

THE PURPOSE OF REVIVAL HAS ALWAYS BEEN TO EMPOWER BELIEVERS TO BE WITNESSES FOR CHRIST.

The Holy Spirit comes to fill us with power so that we can do what Jesus's disciples did when they received the first revival of this age: announce the gospel of the kingdom to the lost; demonstrate God's power with miracles, signs, and wonders; and win people for Christ. If we do not mobilize the church to share the gospel, the ultimate purpose of the revival will be lost.

PRAY FOR THE HARVEST

Remember the order of the end-time cycle: shaking precedes revival, and revival precedes the last-days harvest of souls. Then Jesus will come back! We need to pray to the Lord for the harvest because *"the harvest truly is plentiful, but the laborers are few"* (Matthew 9:37). Revival is God's answer to our prayer that He would *"send out laborers into His harvest"* (verse 38). The end-time revival will awaken God's workers; fill them with His presence; lead them into an intimate relationship with the Father through prayer, worship, and obedience; and ignite within them a fire of passion for the lost who need salvation. The church must be revived to achieve its mission, for its supreme task is the evangelization of the world.

GOD'S ORIGINAL INTENTION FOR THE CHURCH HAS ALWAYS BEEN THE EVANGELIZATION OF THE WORLD.

END-TIME TESTIMONIES

Sara is part of King Jesus Ministry in Miami and has a powerful testimony of a life of prayer and relationship with God. Her son was rescued from drugs by God's hand, without human intervention.

I have witnessed the power of prayer. For sixteen years, my son was addicted to drugs. He even went to jail for his drug use. He led an unstable life; he would get out of prison, only to go back in again. As a mother, I didn't know what to do. I took him to different doctors, even to specialists. It came to the point where they told me they couldn't do anything more for him, saying, "Your son is going to die." But God had other plans. I supernaturally connected with King Jesus Ministry, where I learned about the power of prayer. I began to pray for my son's salvation and to seek more from God. I learned about the power of making a covenant with God, and I began to declare a covenant over my son. During one of many covenants I made, the Holy Spirit said to me, "Stop mourning! Stop crying! It's time to fight for your son's life. Do this for six months." I obeyed that instruction and began to fight for my son's life, believing in the words I had received from the Holy Spirit. At the end of six months, overnight, my son called me and said, "Mom, I don't know why, but I don't want to take drugs anymore." At that moment, I knew that God had set him free and fulfilled His promise.

But the testimony doesn't end there. It turns out that, because of the drugs, my son's teeth were falling out. His gums were rotting. I prayed for him, and now his teeth are completely healthy. God worked a creative miracle. I am immensely grateful. My son was so unstable, and his life was in chaos, yet God showed me His faithfulness. Now my son is a completely different person, healed and serving God, restored to His glory. This was the revival that I was looking for in my family.

Anita Plummer, from Coral Springs, Florida, USA, was diagnosed with a cardiovascular disease that kept her in treatment for seven years. While reading my books, she was freed from spiritual bondage, and, in the process, God healed her physical heart.

In 2012, I was diagnosed with a heart condition. After I had undergone two very difficult surgeries, the doctor finally told me that my condition was incurable. With such news, all that was left for me to do was to trust God. In the midst of this difficult time, someone gave me several books by Apostle Guillermo Maldonado. I began to read them, and then I started to attend church. Little by little, a hunger for the supernatural began to grow within me and cause a great revival in my life. As I progressed in reading the books and attending a House of Peace, God began to speak to me. My mentor prophesied to me, "The next time you go to the doctor, they won't find anything wrong with your heart." I believed that word, and when the day came to go to the doctor—June 25, 2019—the medical report was, "You have a new heart." A new heart! The doctor told me, "It's as if nothing had happened to your heart. There is no disease, no weakening." The blood of Christ and the power of God healed me! It had been an impossible situation, but God is my Healer. Let no one tell you that something is impossible, because nothing is impossible for our God.

CHAPTER 11

THE CONDITIONS FOR REVIVAL

The Holy Spirit is calling to revival those believers in the remnant who long for Christ and His return. (See, for example, Philippians 3:20; 2 Timothy 4:8.) However, there are conditions for this revival to be released. We know that when we do our part, God will faithfully do His part. Therefore, in this concluding chapter, we will review the main conditions that we must fulfill for revival to come to the church of Christ and for there to be an unprecedented harvest for the Lord. Let us consider each of these conditions carefully and prayerfully.

RESPOND TO THE SPIRIT'S CONVICTION

In a previous chapter, we talked about how the influence and manifestation of mankind's moral corruption would substantially increase in the end times. We have seen this development in our day—both in the church and in the world. Moral corruption has led recent generations to be confused about what is good and what is evil. In many aspects of life, what is evil is now called good and vice versa. But the Bible warns us, *"Woe to those who call evil good, and good evil; who put darkness for light, and light for darkness; who put bitter for sweet, and sweet for bitter!"* (Isaiah 5:20).

Today, what the world calls having "freedom of choice" often refers to making a moral choice that openly offends our heavenly Father. The prevailing belief is that people should do what makes them "happy," even if it is abominable to God. This mindset does not take into account whether an action or behavior is sinful. To sin is to violate the law of God, to miss the mark, to twist the path—to grieve God's heart, offending Him in thought, word, and deed.

FREEDOM FROM SIN

How can we become free of sin and have our relationship with God restored? By repenting from our hearts. Remember that to repent is to recognize that we have done something that displeases God and to feel deep conviction that it is wrong and that we cannot continue to do it. Only when we repent from our hearts will we experience real change. That is why, in this time of spiritual darkness, it is important for the church to continue to call sin exactly what it is rather than ignore or disguise it. Otherwise, we will not know we need to repent and receive God's forgiveness.

> *Cry aloud, spare not; lift up your voice like a trumpet; tell My people their transgression, and the house of Jacob their sins.* (Isaiah 58:1)

> *For "whoever calls on the name of the* Lord *shall be saved." How then shall they call on Him in whom they have not believed? And how shall they believe in Him of whom they have not heard? And how shall they hear without a preacher?* (Romans 10:13–14)

Conviction comes to us as the Holy Spirit illuminates our hearts and minds with the truth. (As we will discuss in the next section, after conviction there should be deep repentance.) Without the Holy Spirit, there is no conviction of sin. Whenever the Holy Spirit enlightens our consciences by showing us what is displeasing to God, we must accept His conviction and surrender to His chastening.

As we learned in part I of this book, being under the conviction of the Holy Spirit is not the same as experiencing feelings of guilt or condemnation. Condemnation accuses us, judges us, and leaves us separated from God; and it does not allow us to escape from its viscous cycle. But conviction leads us to a knowledge of our true spiritual state for the purpose of our repentance, restoration with God, and transformation. Again, conviction is often accompanied by a deep feeling of pain in one's heart for having offended and displeased God—and the certainty that one must make an immediate change to be brought back into righteous relationship with Him.

Jesus said of the Holy Spirit, "*When He has come, He will convict the world of sin, and of righteousness, and of judgment: of sin, because they do not believe in Me...*" (John 16:8–9). We must recognize those times when we are being convicted by the precious Spirit of God because, if we do not, our hearts may be hardened, and we will no longer feel that impulse of the Spirit. We are all in a process of surrendering to God certain areas of our lives that do not please Him. Therefore, let us not disregard the voice of the Holy Spirit, or our hearts may fail to hear His warnings.

UNDERGO DEEP REPENTANCE

The church as a whole needs to undergo deep and genuine repentance because, as we discussed earlier, it has been spiritually asleep—adapting to the trends of the world, seeking to please people more than seeking to please God, and attending more to people's emotional demands than to the leading and prompting of the Holy Spirit. Before we explore what repentance is, let's review what repentance is *not*. It is not the same as feeling remorse for something we did that was wrong. Neither is it confessing our sins (although repentance results from our having recognized and confessed our sins). It is not merely a mental decision to change, or an emotional response, such as crying or feeling fearful about the consequences of our sin.

GENUINE REPENTANCE IS A TOTAL CHANGE OF MIND AND HEART AS A RESULT OF SEEING THE GOODNESS OF GOD.

Repentance is something deeper and more decisive than all those reactions to sin. It is the work of the Holy Spirit in our hearts. In the book of Acts, after Peter and John healed the lame man in the name of Jesus at Solomon's Porch, the apostles called the people to repentance, saying, "*Repent therefore and be converted, that your sins may be blotted out, so that times of refreshing may come from the presence of the Lord*" (Acts 3:19). Notice that, in the wording of this verse, repentance precedes conversion; moreover, our sins become blotted out by our repentance.

Spiritually speaking, repentance means a turning away from something that displeases God—sin, iniquity, transgression, evil, unrighteousness. It is the voluntary act of making a U-turn and radically changing direction from following the route of our sins to following the path of the Lord. What Jesus announced to the people of Galilee more than two thousand years ago, He announces to us today: "*The time is fulfilled, and the kingdom of God is at hand. Repent, and believe in the gospel*" (Mark 1:15). The Greek word translated "*repent*" in this verse is *metanoeō*, which means "to think differently or afterwards, i.e. reconsider (moral [sense:] feel compunction) :- repent." Repentance prompted by the Holy Spirit separates us from sin, from transgression, from moral perversion, and from evil; it separates us from everything that saddens and displeases God and that cuts us off from our relationship with Him. "*Or do you despise the riches of His goodness, forbearance, and longsuffering, not knowing that the goodness of God leads you to repentance?*" (Romans 2:4).

REPENTANCE WILL PUT US ON THE PATH TO TRUE CONVERSION, LEADING TO A TOTAL CHANGE OF LIFE.

Part of repentance is confession, because, through confession, we expressly admit our responsibility for our sins, manifest our need for forgiveness in Christ, and declare our willingness to change. The Bible says, "*If we confess our sins, He is faithful and just to forgive us our sins and to cleanse us from all unrighteousness*" (1 John 1:9). After we confess our sins, it is necessary for us to stay away from sin. Our will plays an important role in this process—we have the power to choose how we want to live. No matter how much demonic attack we may experience, we will always have the free will to decide whether we want to give in to sin or resist it, and we have the ability to cry out to God for help. Satan cannot go against our will—our ability to choose curses or blessings, life or death, heaven or hell. Our firm decision to renounce sin and obey God, our genuine repentance, our sincere confession of our sins to God, and our reception of His forgiveness, will take away the devil's right to access and control our lives.

BE CONVERTED

The word *conversion* has a powerful meaning synonymous with *transformation*, which signifies a changing of form. To *transform* means "to change in form, appearance, or structure; metamorphose" or "to change in condition, nature, or character; convert."[101] In terms of the kingdom of God, if we are not transformed, we are not converted. Change is the evidence of conversion. For example, someone may formerly have been angry all the time, but then, after accepting Christ, they begin to exhibit a calm and quiet character, even when wronged, until all their unrighteous anger disappears completely. Or, someone may have been a liar, a drunkard, a drug dealer, an adulterer, a fornicator, or an idolater, but after receiving salvation, they are no longer that type of person; this individual has changed and been transformed into a new person. Such a change signifies that the Holy Spirit brought conviction of sin into their life, and they genuinely repented; as a result, they were converted.

EVIDENCE OF CONVERSION

Thus, true conversion is clearly noticeable in one's character. Until the day the apostle Paul was converted, he persecuted Christians and put them in prison. But, the moment he had a direct encounter with Jesus Christ, his heart was enlightened by the Holy Spirit, he repented of his sins, and his life was completely turned around. He went from persecuting Christians to being persecuted himself for believing in Christ and preaching the same gospel of the kingdom that Jesus preached. When Paul was converted, Jesus sent him to preach to the gentiles (non-Jews, pagans, and foreigners):

> *I now send you* [to the gentiles], *to open their eyes, in order to turn them from darkness to light, and from the power of Satan to God, that they may receive forgiveness of sins and an inheritance among those who are sanctified by faith in Me.* (Acts 26:17–18)

---

101. *Dictionary.com*, s.v. "transform," https://www.dictionary.com/browse/transform.

Paul's passion for, and commitment to, his new life mission reflected the genuineness of his conversion.

WHEN WE SINCERELY REPENT, WE EXPERIENCE TRUE CONVERSION.

FORGIVENESS AND CONVERSION

The Bible teaches us that once God forgives our sins, He forgets them. You may be wondering, "How can an all-knowing God forget our offenses so easily?" The answer is given to us by God Himself in Isaiah 43:25, where He says, *"I, even I, am He who blots out your transgressions for My own sake; and I will not remember your sins."* Additionally, the book of Hebrews explains how Jesus's sacrifice on the cross, by which we were freed from sin, was a sacrifice *"once for all"* (Hebrews 7:27; 9:12; 10:10). Unlike the Old Testament sacrificial system, which commanded that animal sacrifices be offered annually in order to atone for (temporarily cover) the people's sins, Jesus, with His sacrifice on the cross, paid for all the sins of mankind once and for all. We read in Hebrews 10:14, *"For by one offering He has perfected forever those who are being sanctified."* A few verses later, the writer of Hebrews quotes God as saying, *"Their sins and their lawless deeds I will remember no more"* (Hebrews 10:17).

This means that once God forgives our sins, those sins are erased forever. We who were once sinners have now been made righteous by the blood of Christ. This does not mean that we won't sometimes have to pay the consequences of our sins, especially if those sins affected the lives of others. However, it does establish that, before God, we have been cleansed and can once more have a genuine relationship with Him. Once you have been forgiven, do not allow the enemy to accuse you all over again or to bring guilt back into your life. From the moment God forgives you, you are free. The blood of Jesus has erased your transgressions, and you are on your way to true conversion.

However, let me warn you that, although you have been forgiven by God and are free from the oppression of sin, Satan will not easily give up on trying to attack you. In various ways, the enemy will try to turn you back toward your sin. People around you may remind you of your past in order to sow guilt in your heart and to try to convince you that your transformation is a lie. Temptations may come into your life to lead you to fall back into the same old transgressions—or worse sins. But now that you have received Christ, the Holy Spirit lives inside you to empower you, and Jesus stands with you to defend you. (See, for example, Romans 8:26–27; Hebrews 7:25.) No matter what comes against you, you must hold on to the forgiveness God has already given you. You do not need to ask for forgiveness for a sin that has already been forgiven. Remember that when Jesus died, your sins died with Him; and when He rose from the dead, you also rose to new life in Christ.

HUMBLE YOURSELF

Most people consider the act of humbling oneself to have a negative connotation because, in their experience, those who humble themselves are mistreated by their peers and by those in positions of authority, such as parents, teachers, bosses, and rulers. When people are humiliated by the ridicule or abuse of others, this violates the dignity that God Himself has placed inside them as human beings made in His image. Those who have been humiliated in this way find it very difficult to surrender their wills to anyone—including God. They need to realize that the humbleness God asks for as a condition for revival has nothing to do with having their rights trampled on or violated, but rather with their recognizing their need for Him and renouncing their pride, ego, self-will, and arrogance. It means surrendering to God's love and commands, which have been instituted for our good. Unfortunately, many people have built their identities on pride, rather than on the understanding that they are God's children and coheirs with Jesus Christ (see, for example, Romans 8:16–17), and so they resist surrendering to the Lord.

To humble oneself before God is a sign of total dependence on Him. It is an act of the will—and it is the entryway into God's presence. There is no substitute for humbleness because *"God resists the proud, but gives grace* to the humble" (James 4:6). Thus, for many people, the greatest obstacle to repentance is their woundedness and pride; to them, to humble themselves is an act of weakness. Pride hides from us our true condition because we want to preserve a false image of ourselves at any price. Yet God—who completely knows us and understands how we function, because He created us—wants us to humble ourselves voluntarily. That is the key to being forgiven, to comprehending and receiving our identity as God's children, and to living in true and complete freedom.

HUMBLENESS WILL ALWAYS ATTRACT GOD, WHILE PRIDE WILL DRIVE HIM AWAY.

The best way to humble yourself is to examine your heart and recognize your own prideful condition. As described earlier, when people will not humble themselves, God Himself will humble them, "*for whoever exalts himself will be humbled, and he who humbles himself will be exalted*" (Luke 14:11). Such humbling by God will occur not only within the church, but also in the world among the unrepentant. Those who have rejected the Messiah will not be taken by Him in the rapture and will suffer the judgment at His second coming. Therefore, *this is the time to choose* between eternal death and the abundant life that God offers us. If we want revival that leads to salvation, restoration, and true conversion, we must shed our pride and humble ourselves before God so that He can heal our hearts and fully transform us.

DEVELOP DIVINE HUNGER

Are you satisfied with traditional Christianity, or do you long for revival? Are you content with reading the Bible as a history book, or are you hungry for revelation from the living Word? If you want religion and tradition, there is plenty of both in the world, but I warn you that they will keep you in a dead spiritual atmosphere. To receive a revival of the Holy Spirit, we must be spiritually hungry. God will not pour out His Spirit over people who do not desperately yearn for His presence. Sadly, I must admit that I have not yet seen intense spiritual hunger among believers, except on a few occasions. People must know that revival does not come by faith alone—merely believing it can happen. If you review the summary of historical revivals in chapter 7, you will note that each revival began with people who were hungry for God; people who cried out, prayed, fasted, and paid a high spiritual price to see that revival. Such hunger increases our capacity to be filled with the Holy Spirit; it leads us to perform desperate acts to draw near to God, to pay a price we never imagined paying, to give up everything in order to experience an outpouring from heaven.

ONLY A DESPERATE HUNGER FOR THE MANIFESTATION OF THE HOLY SPIRIT WILL BRING THE END-TIME REVIVAL TO OUR GENERATION.

PRAY AND FAST

The origin of practically everything God works among His people on earth is found in prayer and fasting. Prayer is like a magnet that attracts all that God wants to give His children. It is also what will bring the greatest revival in history since the outpouring of the Spirit at Pentecost. And prayer is what will accelerate the time of Jesus's appearing.

It is time to pray, fast, and humble ourselves in the presence of the Lord! Our prayers will not come back empty; rather, they will move heaven on our behalf. The Bible is filled with examples of supernatural moves that were provoked by prayer. For instance, when Joshua prayed, *"the sun stood still"* until he defeated his enemies. (See Joshua 10:12–13.) When Elijah prayed, fire came down from heaven and consumed the burnt offering, and the prophets of the false god Baal were defeated (see 1 Kings 18:30–40); then, with the prophet's intercession, God sent a *"heavy rain"* to end a time of severe drought (see 1 Kings 18:41–46). Jesus prayed to the Father for His disciples to be kept from the wiles of the world (see John 17:9–11), and there are innumerable examples of the answer to His prayer throughout history to this very day.

THE GREAT END-TIME REVIVAL WILL COME WHEN THE CHURCH BENDS ITS KNEES IN PRAYER AND FASTING.

SEEK HIGH PRAISE AND WORSHIP

Many believers are unaware of the divine principle that God moves first in the dimension of sound. To put it simply, the entire universe was created at the command of God's voice, and the sound of His voice will always precede His work. That is why the type of praise that Christians engage in when they gather together for worship is important. God wants us to play and sing melodies from His Word and His Spirit that will bring the atmosphere of heaven to earth, that will carry the sound of revival. Therefore, we must remove the old atmosphere that is charged with melancholy from the past and bring in a new atmosphere where the Holy Spirit can move in freedom.

Past victories are good, but they are gone now. Today, God is doing a new thing! There are new souls to win and new territories to conquer for the kingdom of God. Our praise and worship cannot be conventional, ritualistic, dull, or flat. On the contrary, it must consist of new spiritual songs and prophetic content that will release the movement of the Spirit among His people; praise and worship that will always be in ascension, leading people into the presence of God and bringing His presence to people by inviting an outpouring of the Spirit. This is high praise and worship that will lead to revival.

GOD MOVES IN THE DIMENSION OF SOUND, AND THE UNIVERSE WAS CREATED AT THE SOUND OF HIS VOICE.

MAKE PROPHETIC DECLARATIONS

As I indicated earlier, all movements of the Spirit require the construction of a spiritual atmosphere. This occurs not only through our prayers, fasting, and worship, but also through our prophetic declarations. All of these elements, together, create a momentum or spiritual impulse that, at its climax, activates revival. When we continually speak prophetic declarations from the Word of God and the revelation of His Spirit, these declarations accumulate like a mass of spiritual power. The more people feed that atmosphere, the closer we come to an outpouring. When the cup of prayer, fasting, worship, and prophecy reaches its peak, inevitably, there will be an outpouring of the Spirit and something new will come.

THE ATMOSPHERE MUST BE CONDUCIVE TO THE SPIRIT OF GOD FOR THERE TO BE REVIVAL.

Every spiritual atmosphere that we build must be conducive to revival. If it isn't, the Holy Spirit will not move in awakening. In a sense, the church has to provoke revival by being assertive in prayer, intercession, praise, worship, and prophetic declarations. Prophetic proclamations from the Spirit in the now—in addition to declarations of biblical prophecy and prophecy through the centuries that have yet to be fulfilled—will prompt the end-time revival and the coming of Christ, *"whom heaven must receive until the times of restoration of all things, which God has spoken by the mouth of all His holy prophets since the world began"* (Acts 3:21).

TIMES OF REFRESHING

Let us return to the theme of Acts 3:19: *"Repent therefore and be converted, that your sins may be blotted out, so that times of refreshing may come from the presence of the Lord."* The phrase "blot out" means "to obliterate" or "to wipe out of existence or memory."[102] It indicates making something disappear completely. When we repent, the Lord erases all our sins, and we become new creations in His presence. *"Times of refreshing"* refers to a state of absolute trust and rest in God's presence.

God is restoring His presence in the midst of His people. The Greek word translated *"refreshing"* in the above verse is *anapsyxis*, which means "a

---

102. *Dictionary.com*, s.v. "blot out," https://www.dictionary.com/browse/blot--out.

recovery of breath, i.e. (figurative) *revival.*" When we repent and experience true conversion, times of refreshment, revival, and rest come to our personal, family, and ministry lives. Thus, during the end times, the church will be at rest, while the world is in turmoil and confusion.

It is time to yield to every conviction the Holy Spirit brings to our hearts. If we do not repent of our transgressions and iniquity, we will continue in a cycle of sin. Do you hold in your heart a deep feeling of having offended God? What personal or family sin might the Holy Spirit be bringing to your mind and heart so that you can repent of it at this time? I pray to the Lord that His Holy Spirit will enlighten your conscience and bring conviction of sin. When this happens, surrender to that conviction, repent, confess your sin, and turn to the Lord. That is the condition for God to bring revival into your life, which includes the *"times of refreshing"* promised in His Word.

END-TIME TESTIMONIES

A few years ago, after much prayer, the Lord opened doors for us to bring to South Africa the revival that is occurring in our ministry. Among the thousands of testimonies that we heard and recorded there, I want to share those of two young men who were activated not only by the teachings and impartations of the supernatural power of God through our direct ministry in their country, but also through our discipleship materials, such as books and videos. After spending years in spiritually dry churches, they were finally able to see God's power flow through their lives.

My name is Pastor Wayne, and I have seen God work miracles, signs, and wonders. He has done so much through the prayerful seeking of the members of our congregation that it has all been an experience that has completely changed my perspective on the supernatural. We have been teaching King Jesus Ministry materials in our prayer meetings. As a result, we have been able to experience not only the power of God, but also something tangible of what He is doing. One day, I prayed at the edge of a river that had been dry for over fifty years, and, two months later, the river was filled with water. God has really outdone Himself, and we have been able to see the power of His love for His people.

My name is Petrus Mashwele, and I am very grateful to God for all that He has done. I have been able to witness His power over His people in a new dimension, which has truly caused a great awakening. I was attending a church that was dead, but then many of the members had an encounter with God, and a new wave of His power came. After we read Apostle Guillermo Maldonado's books, we were activated to move in the supernatural. For example, there was the case of a person we ministered to who was healed of HIV by the power of God. In another example, a woman who had no fallopian tubes was enabled to conceive. Today, she has a baby in her arms thanks to our prayers and our belief that God can perform miracles. There have been so many miracles, signs, and wonders! It is great to see that God still heals people! We are thankful to be part of this movement and are looking forward to the great revival that is to come.

Apostle Israel Daniels and his wife, Courtney, were living in the United States when God called them to plant a ministry in South Africa. Following that move, they connected with our ministry and began to see revival and transformation manifest in their ministry. Tremendous things are happening in their region of the world.

My name is Israel Daniels. I used to be a Muslim, but the Lord saved me and took me out of that religion. Seven years ago, the Lord told my wife and me to move to Cape Town, South Africa, which is located on the southwest coast of the country. We went in obedience to God, and supernatural things began to happen, including miracles and a change in our ministry. Suddenly, people with AIDS were being healed. We have the before-and-after documentation!

Seven months ago, the Lord spoke to us while we were praying and fasting. He told us that, at this point in our ministry, and because of the nations He was giving us to be won for the gospel, we needed to submit to a spiritual covering. So, we went to King Jesus Ministry seeking the covering of Apostle Maldonado. After we connected with the apostle's ministry through the Internet, we began to notice a difference.

One day, my wife and I were watching the University of the Supernatural Ministry[103] online in our bedroom. At one point, Apostle Maldonado was ministering, and he said, "Places, people, and things will respond to you." We were receiving revelation from the presence of God, and suddenly I shouted, "Kenya!" My wife thought we were going to travel to Kenya. Four days later, I received a message through Facebook from someone who told me that he had been looking at our posts, and that he had properties in Kenya (schools, hospitals, and more). All we had to do was plant a church there. My wife and I went to Kenya a few months ago, and, to the glory of God, we are planting a church there. God is giving us the nations. We've seen His radical movement in King Jesus Ministry, and we've taken that revival to several countries.

---

103. A three-day event that King Jesus Ministry hosts several times a year to train leaders from all over the world in the supernatural power of God.

CONCLUSION: A TIME OF CONSECRATION

We are living in times of shaking that will lead to an unprecedented move of the Holy Spirit in revival and tremendous manifestations of God's glory. In the world today, we are seeing the fulfillment of end-time signs— such as plagues (epidemics and pandemics) and wars and rumors of war— that point to God's judgment and the coming of the Lord. However, for the church of Christ, the signs that point to the Lord's coming are different from these others; they include *"times of refreshing"* (Acts 3:19) and great revivals and harvests. For the church, Christ comes as Redeemer; but for the world, He comes as Judge.

I pray that each person reading this book will begin to walk in obedience to God's holy Word. I pray that you will walk in the fear of the Lord. I pray that the heavenly Father will establish you as a witness for Him in the end times and that you will receive a revival in your life and in the life of your community and nation like you have never experienced before.

Today, I prophesy that there will be various types of portals over the United States and other parts of the world. In some places, there will be a huge portal that covers a large geographical area; in other places, there will be a smaller portal like a door; in still others, the portal will be an individual believer. The important thing is that these portals will give people access to the Source from which the power of the resurrection flows. The

Holy Spirit will do sovereign acts of God, releasing revival in many places at the same time. Wherever there are portals in any form, there will be open heavens through which God's power will flow in revival.

I see in the Spirit that God's light in those places of revival will grow; then, that light will begin to multiply. Suddenly, every state in the United States will have the manifestation of a facet of the Holy Spirit. There will be different emphases according to the particular place and people, which will make each revival distinct. They won't be uniform or methodical. I see that, at the end of this final revival of the church age, the individual lights will suddenly converge in one place, and every believer in the remnant will become one in the Spirit and in His divine power. This end-time revival will be global. Again, it will not be like other revivals but will be something totally new.

REVIVAL WILL RESTORE US COMPLETELY TO THE PRESENCE OF GOD AND RENEW OUR RELATIONSHIP WITH HIM.

THE ROAR OF REVIVAL

Recently, the prophet Tracy Cooke gave King Jesus Ministry a word from God:

I saw a lot of buses after buses coming to the church; they were pulling in. I saw thousands of people coming in; they were so many that they couldn't get in; there was no more room in the temple. In the vision, the Lord showed that you have to look for another venue. I saw the Lion of Judah roaring inside the temple. There was a cloud over the people. The words are changing over this house. The breath of the Holy Spirit is blowing. The Lord said, "I am roaring from this house to the entire world. I am roaring revival in this house." Inside the church, I saw [His] hand like a cloud. For some reason, [it] hit the right side stronger than the left side. I saw three angels coming closer to the altar. The power was getting stronger, and the people were getting financial breakthrough. God was doing something with their families.

This vision of revival will take months or perhaps years to materialize. It is our job to prepare for end-time revival through repentance, prayer, worship, offerings, and so on. God gave us this vision and prophetic word to bring revival from heaven to earth through prayer. Therefore, for us, these are times of consecration, fasting, and seeking the Lord, because we want our church to be a portal of revival for the United States and for many other cities and nations of the earth. You, also, have a calling to prepare for the last-days revival, to follow what the Lord leads you to do, and to consecrate your life to prepare for the return of the Lord!

PRAYER OF RESTORATION

If you are interested in spiritual matters but have not yet identified yourself as being part of the bride of Christ—if hurt, bitterness, or distractions have driven you away from the house of God—today, the Lord wants to heal your heart and restore you as a member of His chosen remnant. Why does your heart need to be healed? Because if you are not open to being transformed, the condition of your life will become worse. *"He who is unjust, let him be unjust still; he who is filthy, let him be filthy still; he who is righteous, let him be righteous still; he who is holy, let him be holy still"* (Revelation 22:11).

The Holy Spirit brings us moments of conviction to reveal our spiritual state and lead us to repentance and conversion. If you recognize that you have turned away from God, your heavenly Father is calling you and waiting for you with open arms, ready to forgive you, heal you, and fill you with His Spirit. If you will not admit that you are estranged from God, or you refuse to change your sinful ways, then your stubborn will is in the way of the restoration you need; you are blocking God's work in your life. If you prefer to give in to temptation, that is a sign that you are moving away from the Lord, because the devil can only tempt you with what he sees that you want. When people begin to compromise their principles, sin comes easily. If they continue to commit the same sins, telling themselves that doing so doesn't matter, they are turning away from God's presence and His calling for their lives. No practicing sinner can enter heaven. If you believe that you are saved but are unconcerned about sinning, you have fallen into a delusion; your conscience is seared because you have no resistance to evil. You have compromised the truth and need to repent now! Remember, if you do not judge yourself, you will be judged by God later, and there will be no opportunity for repentance. Now is the time!

Let me say a prayer over you now:

Father, in the name of Jesus, I bind the enemy spirits that lead Your children to turn away from You, to stray from Your holiness and truth. I bind the spirits of lust, perversion, and rebellion. I release the wills and emotions of Your children from their influence by the flesh and by the enemy. I break all negative influences over their souls. I bind the spirits that are in the environments of their homes, their family relationships, and all their other associations. I bind the work of iniquity in their lives; I bind the spirit of pride and the spirit that rebels against truth in their souls. Be broken! Be broken! Be broken, in the name of Jesus! I loose every reader from the captivity they have been wrestling with. And now, I release in them a holy zeal for the truth so that they may not compromise the principles of the kingdom. I loose them in the name of Jesus. The devil's strategies to drive them away from You have been annulled.

Holy Spirit, come with fresh oil now and touch every part of their lives that they have not yet surrendered to you. Touch their hearts, Lord. I declare that, from this day on, they will stop turning away from You and return to Your arms and Your presence. Amen!

God will repair every area of your soul that has been wounded. He will revive your spirit and cause you to be part of the remnant, that glorious church for which Christ will soon come. I urge you to seek the presence of almighty God, to walk soberly in holiness, and to live righteously before the Lord. I pray that you would passionately desire to please God and that you would intercede for Him to bring the final revival of the Holy Spirit upon all the peoples of the earth, so that *"every knee* [will] *bow,...and that every tongue* [will] *confess that Jesus Christ is Lord, to the glory of God the Father*" (Philippians 2:10–11), and so that "*the kingdoms of this world* [will] *become the kingdoms of our Lord and of His Christ, and He shall reign forever and ever!*" (Revelation 11:15). Amen!

ABOUT THE AUTHOR

Apostle Guillermo Maldonado is the senior pastor and founder of King Jesus International Ministry (Ministerio Internacional El Rey Jesus) in Miami, Florida, a multicultural church considered to be one of the fastest growing in the United States. King Jesus Ministry, whose foundation is built upon the Word of God, prayer, and worship, currently has a membership of more than 18,000 in the United States, including the main church in Miami, its campuses, its daughter churches, and its online church. Apostle Maldonado is also a spiritual father to more than 400 churches in 60 countries throughout the United States, Latin America, Europe, Africa, Asia, and New Zealand, which form the Supernatural Global Network, representing more than 705,000 people. In addition, he is the founder of the University of the Supernatural Ministry (USM). The building of kingdom leaders and the visible manifestations of God's supernatural power distinguish the ministry as the number of its members constantly multiplies.

A national best-selling author, Apostle Maldonado has written over fifty books and manuals, many of which have been translated into other languages. His books with Whitaker House include *Jesus Is Coming Soon, Created for Purpose, Breakthrough Prayer, Breakthrough Fast, Stress-Free Living, How to Walk in the Supernatural Power of God, The Glory of God, The Kingdom of Power, Supernatural Transformation, Supernatural Deliverance,* and *Divine Encounter with the Holy Spirit,* all of which are available in both English and Spanish. In addition, he preaches the message of Jesus Christ and His redemptive power on his international television program, *The Supernatural Now* (*Lo sobrenatural ahora*). Apostle Maldonado has a doctorate in Christian counseling from Vision International University and a master's degree in practical theology from Oral Roberts University.

Be a friend of King Jesus Ministry and *be part* of the supernatural movement that is the bridge between *hope* and hopelessness.

supernaturalpartners.org

(305) 382-3171 ext. 3

Welcome to Our House!

We Have a Special Gift for You

It is our privilege and pleasure to share in your love of Christian books. We are committed to bringing you authors and books that feed, challenge, and enrich your faith.

To show our appreciation, we invite you to sign up to receive a specially selected **Reader Appreciation Gift**, with our compliments. Just go to the Web address at the bottom of this page.

God bless you as you seek a deeper walk with Him!

whpub.me/nonfictionthx

WHITAKER
HOUSE